Cambridge Elements ☰

**Elements in Histories of Emotions
and the Senses**
edited by
Jan Plamper
Goldsmiths, University of London

SATIRE AND THE PUBLIC EMOTIONS

Robert Phiddian

Flinders University

CAMBRIDGE
UNIVERSITY PRESS

CAMBRIDGE
UNIVERSITY PRESS

University Printing House, Cambridge CB2 8BS, United Kingdom

One Liberty Plaza, 20th Floor, New York, NY 10006, USA

477 Williamstown Road, Port Melbourne, VIC 3207, Australia

314–321, 3rd Floor, Plot 3, Splendor Forum, Jasola District Centre,
New Delhi – 110025, India

79 Anson Road, #06–04/06, Singapore 079906

Cambridge University Press is part of the University of Cambridge.

It furthers the University's mission by disseminating knowledge in the pursuit of
education, learning, and research at the highest international levels of excellence.

www.cambridge.org
Information on this title: www.cambridge.org/9781108798839
DOI: 10.1017/9781108869263

First published 2019

A catalogue record for this publication is available from the British Library.

ISBN 978-1-108-79883-9 (paperback)
ISSN 2632-1068 (online)
ISSN 2632-105X (print)

Satire and the Public Emotions

Elements in Histories of Emotions and the Senses

DOI: 10.1017/9781108869263
First published online: December 2019

Robert Phiddian
Flinders University

Author for correspondence: Robert Phiddian, robert.phiddian@flinders.edu.au

Abstract: The dream of political satire – to fearlessly speak truth to power – is not matched by its actual effects. This Element explores the role of satirical communication in licensing public expression of harsh emotions defined in neuroscience as the CAD (Contempt, Anger, Disgust) triad. The mobilisation of these emotions is a fundamental distinction between satirical and comic laughter. Phiddian pursues this argument particularly through an account of Jonathan Swift and his contemporaries. They played a crucial role in the early eighteenth century to make space in the public sphere for intemperate dissent, an essential condition of free political expression.

Keywords: political satire, CAD (Contempt, Anger, Disgust) triad of emotions, Jonathan Swift, *Gulliver's Travels*, eighteenth-century satire, comedy and laughter

ISBNs: 9781108798839 (PB), 9781108869263 (OC)
ISSNs: 2632-1068 (online), 2632-105X (print)

Contents

Prologue: The Beginning of Political Satire

You are at the Festival of the Lenaea in Ancient Athens, 424 BCE, watching the *Knights*, a new play by Aristophanes. Most of the city's citizens are there in the massive Theatre of Dionysus. Two masked actors come forward and, after some coarse dialogue, Demosthenes holds forth about their master Demos, and then about Paphlagon, a recently purchased slave:

> We two have got a master
> with a countryman's bad temper; he's a peasant, very quick to anger –
> Demos of the Pnyx, an irritable, deaf,
> puny old man. And last new moon
> he bought a slave, the tanner Paphlagon,
> a total scumbag who will slander anyone.

There is already some laughter among a few dozen of the thousands at the theatre. It grows and takes on a harsh edge as Demosthenes continues:

> He quickly worked out what the old man's like,
> and falling at his master's feet he fawned
> and flattered and deceived his boss
> with little scraps of leather, saying things like this –
> 'Oh Demos, only try one case before you have your bath,'
> 'eat this,' 'quaff that,' 'enjoy this sweet,' and 'take these twenty
> bucks.' 'D'you want a late night snack?' And then this Paphlagon
> would grab some food that we'd prepared and give it to
> our master as *his* gift.

People are looking as much towards the best benches in the theatre as at the stage. Why?

> He shuts us out and won't let any other slave
> wait on our master; he has got a leather strap, and when
> Demos is dining he drives all the politicians off.
> He tells the old man oracles – and Demos laps them up.
> He's realized the old man is a fool,
> so this is what he does. He slanders everyone inside the house
> with outright lies; then we get whipped while Paphlagon
> goes round to all the servants, makes demands,
> harasses them, takes bribes, and says:
> 'D'you see Hylas is getting flogged – and all because of me?
> Keep in with me, or you will die this very day.'

Everyone is looking now at Cleon, because those last words were done in a very passable imitation of his public voice. Demosthenes continues, first bitterly then anxiously:

> And so we pay him; if we don't, we will be beaten up
> by the old man and shit ourselves eight times. . . .
> Nothing gets past Paphlagon.
> His eyes are watching everywhere; he's got one foot
> in Pylos, and the other's here, in the Assembly. So
> his arse is gaping wide, his hands are forcing
> people to pay bribes, his mind is bent on theft.[1]
>
>   *(Aristophanes, 2011: 94–5)*

Cleon, the most prominent citizen and general in Athens, stands. He takes the applause and the raucous laughter with a big if rather fixed grin and bends over to show that his arse is properly clothed. Then he sits down to watch a play which continues to excoriate him and goes on to win the prize for best comedy in the Festival.

*****

We can never know if it happened like this, or whether Cleon was there at all, but the play was staged at the Lenaea and did win the prize. Robert Elliott (1960: 15) uses the semi-mythological Archilocus, a bard in Archaic Greece whose invectives are said literally to have killed some of his targets, as 'crucial for an understanding of the image of the satirist'. In a similar spirit, I present this tableau of confrontation between Aristophanes and Cleon as a central trope for political satire, with the force of an originating myth. There, before the *polis* yet licensed by laughter, satire arraigns a powerful demagogue for corruption. Cleon cannot lash out without loss of face, and yet the ridicule in the public laughter channels disgust, anger, and contempt at his work and status. Apparently, Cleon had complained about Aristophanes' earlier (now lost) *Babylonians* (426 BCE) and begun legal proceedings, so he got everything thrown at him at the next opportunity (Robson, 2009: 3). A satirist must take a risk and be sufficiently supported by public acclaim that the authorities or the affronted think twice about repressing the gadfly.

Anyone with an appetite for satire wants this scenario to be true because it is so emotionally satisfying. That, in its simplest form, is why an account of satire involves a history of the public emotions. Within the play-frame of fiction and spectacle, a satirist can attack a public figure with impunity and channel hostility towards him. Aristophanes also indulges in punning scatology on place names that Ewans renders suggestively with 'his arse is gaping wide' while he squeezes bribes from the innocent.[2] It is a carnival of public disgust, exacting condign punishment on the palpably guilty. Or it is seditious libel. Or it is just a joke.

---

[1] A handful of lines have been omitted for dramatic flow.
[2] Ewans discusses the language play in this passage in his introduction, Aristophanes, 2011: 32–33.

And the public, Demos, does not escape unscathed. As so often in satire, it is lazy and self-indulgent – too easily seduced by grasping buffoons like Cleon/ Paphlagon and their progeny down the centuries. It needs to be prodded and discomforted, to resist populism and rise to the charismatic wisdom required by the satirist. For, in this enthusiastic myth, the satirist is, *pace* John Belushi in *Blues Brothers* (1980), on a mission from God. No one put it higher than Alexander Pope, 'O sacred weapon! Left for Truth's defence, / Sole Dread of Folly, Vice, and Insolence!' (*Epilogue to the Satires*, II, l. 212–13, 1963). In reality, things prove more complex and conflicted than this, of course. Nevertheless, Aristophanes' and Pope's powerful desire to achieve some harsh poetic justice in a world of knaves and fools lies at the root of the satiric mode. Satire is impassioned rhetoric that claims to serve the public good. This Element addresses those broadly political passions and their effects in the world.

Section 1 moves from the myth of impertinent efficacy just outlined to ask more rigorously what functions satires can be seen to serve. The result of this wide survey is not cheering for those who dream of satirists being respected as prophets, but it does suggest that satirical interventions can have an unpredictable range of political and cultural effects. Section 2 drills down into my central theoretical proposition, that a primary function of satires is to mobilise the CAD triad of public emotions – contempt, anger, and disgust. This requires engagement with neuroscientific and philosophical research and raises some essentially ethical questions about the validity of satire as a form of public shaming and rhetorical aggression. Section 3 explores a formative historical case study of British satire in the 1720s and 1730s. It argues that satire played a crucial role in making room for oppositional and intemperate passions in the cultural and political stability that developed during Sir Robert Walpole's long primacy. The presence of more or less tolerated satire is one of the most reliable signs of the freeish public expression experienced by some of the peoples some of the time since the eighteenth century. Finally, in Section 4, I seek to bring these theoretical and historical threads together in a reading of Jonathan Swift's *Gulliver's Travels*. I want, above all, to revive a sense of this now canonical satire's volatility in its cultural and political moment, to imagine some of the reactions it provoked when it was still possible that it might be suppressed as sedition.

While *Satire and the Public Emotions* concentrates on 'hyper-canonical' literary British satirists of the early eighteenth century (Greenberg 2018: 18), it is also informed by a parallel body of scholarship on contemporary Australian political cartooning.[3] This work, a collaboration with Haydon Manning from my university's Politics Department, has been crucial for me in shifting

---

[3] See Phiddian and Manning, 2008, and more than a dozen co-authored articles since 1998.

attention to the effects rather than the meanings of satires. Thus I hope that the argument about satire and its mobilisation of the harsh emotions of contempt, anger, and disgust can be sensibly modified by readers and applied to other contexts than the one I argue it through in detail here. The emotional dynamics of what Swift, Pope and John Gay do with Walpole are, for this project, recognisably similar to Aristophanes' attack on Cleo, or *Saturday Night Live*'s disapprobation of President Trump. There has been a historicist turn in literary studies, especially of the eighteenth century, one that values specificity, difference, and archival discovery. My study of satire is not historicist in that sense; instead, it takes an orientation from the history of emotions which permits some generalisation across time and place concerning rhetorical forms and public passions. The format of this Cambridge Elements series allows me to write this as a long essay rather than a treatise: to propose these ideas and to outline them plausibly but by no means definitively. If readers are provoked to find other contexts where this account of satire works, hits limits, or needs to be contested, the Element will have fulfilled its purpose.

1 The Functions of Satire

Satire and Reception

For a couple of decades now, I have been trying to work out what satire does – not the single essential thing that a text must do to deserve entry to a pure category of 'satire', but the range of things that texts recognised as satirical often enough do. This is a messy, empirical business, rather than *a priori* theorising. It does not belong to any single discipline, which has led me to dissatisfaction with the formal definitions of satire that literary studies developed in the twentieth century. Unless you confine the genre to poems in the manner of Horace, Juvenal, and Pope's 'satires', form is a second-order issue in addressing satire. It is better understood as a mode rather than a genre, an aspect of some texts which allows for the expression of hostile attitudes and emotions towards figures, practices, and institutions of public significance. Indeed, satire is not intrinsically literary at all, and its 'capture' by literary theory was already a problem before the deconstructive doctrine of the 'death of the author' further compounded the situation by making recourse to any projection of intention 'problematic.' Certainly what readers and audiences make of satires is a more important object of study than pure and irretrievable authorial intentions. However, what we make of satirical texts depends on a perception of satirical purpose and deconstructive readings are almost hardwired to refuse to apprehend this.[4]

---

[4] I argue this case against formalist approaches at length in Phiddian, 2013.

Thus it is better to understand satire as a mode that can appear in a wide range of texts, one that generally seeks to evoke hostile laughter for critical purposes. Indeed, the noun 'satire' is really only a descriptive label for a text (novel, chat show, poem, cartoon, painting, and so on) where the satirical mode reaches a critical mass such as to become dominant. Paul Simpson (2003: 51) has argued that 'satire, as an everyday mode of discourse, is more endemic and more outside anything approaching "high culture" than ... many critics appear to realize.' He concludes his critique of existing scholarship with the proposition that satire

> is a complexly interdiscursive mode of communication. It is also a mode of communication that, frankly, does not sit easily beside forms of literary discourse such as poems, plays or prose, but which nonetheless seems to have been totally appropriated into literary study. The critics thus inherited a term which could only marginally be aligned with literary writing, but aligned it had to be, which may explain the consistent attempts to canonize, subsume and genericize this type of discourse. To some extent, satire needs to be wrested away from 'Literature' and to be put instead in the context of popular and populist discourses. (Simpson, 2003: 62)

The literary-theoretical tendency to 'genericize', to describe satire as an entity, exists despite the fact that very few texts, in whatever media, can usefully be described formally as satires.[5] Where satirical purpose becomes dominant is a judgement that will vary between readers or viewers because it is an emotional as well as a formal judgement, but most people would agree to call *Gulliver's Travels* (1726) a satire and *Bleak House* (1853) a realist novel with satirical elements, not a satire. Simply recalling Evelyn Waugh's *Loved One* (1948) or Margaret Atwood's *The Handmaid's Tale* (1985), however, suggests that categorical distinctions in this field will always be rubbery and, I wish to add, finally academic in the negative sense. If a conservative Christian interpreted *The Colbert Report* as unironic public commentary, despite framing as satire that no liberal viewer could miss, that is a fact a scholar has to attend to, not simply an error to be ridiculed. For her, Colbert simply has not worked as satire, but as something else (Baumgartner and Morris, 2008; Lamarre, Landreville, and Beam, 2009).

What makes something satirical 'in the world' is the perception in an audience of satirical purpose. Moreover, there is no guarantee that different spectators will deduce the same purpose from the same text, or the purpose

---

[5] See Condren, 2012. 'Menippean' is a label applied to many such satires but either it is so capacious a term as to include all things satirical, or it requires a meticulous process of exclusions that create more problems than they solve. It has very limited utility for my argument; see Weinbrot, 2005; Musgrave, 2014; McLuhan, 2015.

consciously intended by the author. Construing the purpose(s) of satirical texts depends on temperamental and ideological predisposition in the spectators; this is politically more important than hermeneutic acumen, as can be seen in the controversies surrounding *causes célèbres* such as *The Satanic Verses* (1988) or the Danish cartoons of Mohammed.[6] The interesting political questions in the analysis of satirical texts concern what spectators make of them, and how they react, not whether they get them 'right'. This is especially the case when satires successfully provoke high levels of controversy. Thus I am interested in the consequences of satirical texts, including the unintended consequences. So, the question for this Element is not what do *The Beggar's Opera* (1728) or the *Jyllands-Posten* cartoons mean so much as what do they do? What is the function of these texts in the developing political and press ecology of early Georgian Britain or the twenty-first century's brave new world of digital circulation (so personal and so global)? What emotional work occurs? The overt critical aim of satire is calling out knaves and fools to demand cultural, social, or political change, but history provides few examples of this working in a direct or instrumental way. There has been vastly more satire than there has been change caused by the correct understanding of satire. Consequently, it seems worthwhile to explore what other cultural and emotional work satire and the types of laughter it licenses do.

Satire and Emotion

One of the things satires nearly always do is express, evoke, and provoke indignation. This works for the authors, no doubt, but the more significant expression of indignation occurs in the audience, where different expressions of public indignation are mobilised or performed. 'Indignation' is a convenient umbrella word because it can be traced back as far as Swift's credo of *saeva indignatio* (savage indignation) expressed in his epitaph (Phiddian, 2016), and it is as current as the post–financial crisis phenomenon of Stéphane Hessel's *Indignez-vous* (2010) and protests by the *Indignados* in Spain. Among modern psychological studies of the emotions, however, it is not a term in common use, and the words it maps most closely onto are the CAD triad of negative emotions: contempt, anger, and disgust.[7] The satirical and the purely comic elements of texts can share tropes and techniques such as caricature, incongruity, and irony, but the main, transhistorical difference between them is the engagement of these visceral emotions in satire. Indeed, a novel like Orwell's *1984* (1949) or the haunting critique of globalisation from the 1990s by John Spooner (1999;

---

[6] See Appignanesi and Maitland, 1990; Ruthven, 1990; Klausen, 2009.
[7] See Rozin et al., 1999 and Section 2.

GLOBALISATION

Figure 1 John Spooner, *A Spooner in the works: the art of John Spooner* (Melbourne: Text Publishing 1999), reproduced with permission.

Figure 1) can be satirical without being funny at all. Satirical caricature and distortion are often comical, but they need not be.

While the detailed analysis in this Element is set mainly in the 1720s and 1730s, its resonance need not stop there. I want to map the CAD triad onto satirical texts in a way that respects historical difference in specifics without so making a fetish of historicism as to deny broad similarities of emotional experience across time and place. I certainly do not present twenty-first-century neuroscience as a neat solution to all satirical affect – behavioural psychology can exhibit grandly synchronic ambitions to explain human consciousness scientifically and universally but is only narrowly true of the populations of mostly North American university students who answer ethically cleared surveys and get wired up to functional magnetic resonance imaging (fMRI) machines. This distinctive subject group has snidely but accurately been characterised as WEIRD, that is, Western Educated Industrialised Rich Democratic (Henrich, Heine, and Norenzayan, 2010; Haidt, 2012). Their experiences of contempt, anger, and disgust will be culturally inflected in ways different from the original spectators of Swift and his Scriblerian colleagues, but it is extremely probable that there will be broad similarities that we can learn from and extend to other, non-literary satirical phenomena. I am neither a 'basic emotions' universalist nor a historicist particularist.[8] My ambition is to project an extensive view of satire without attempting the unmanageable (and inevitably tedious) task of being comprehensive across time and place.

Some studies in cognitive psychology, stylistics, and media have begun to explore who gets satires, how, and why.[9] Literary studies of satire have also gestured towards a more transactional view of satire than was evident in the formal concerns of the past, with Charles Knight (2004) talking of 'the satiric frame of mind'; Melinda Rabb (2007: 12) of 'getting irony'; and Ashley Marshall (2013) insisting both that temperament influences satire and that 'tone matters'. However, little will be gained if we leap from the sophisticated cultural constructivism of literary analysis to a reductive scientism that involves wiring a statistically significant number of subjects up to fRMI scanners while watching *The Colbert Report* or reading the *Modest Proposal* to show which parts of the brain fire when satire is received. There is a body of behavioural psychological research of this kind into humour, and it has a degree of validity precisely because the cognitive experience of a joke can be abstracted substantially from cultural context into something approaching pure emotional reaction. Satirical responses are, perforce, much more contextually and historically situated than that. The image of Winnie the Pooh has had widespread humorous import for almost a century in the English-speaking world and beyond. Since 2017 in China, however, these images have been suppressed by the authorities as far as is possible on the Internet because of satirical play on a resemblance between the bear of little brain and supreme leader Xi Jinping. At the moment of writing, an orange hairpiece has almost planet-wide recognition as a satirical marker, but that may not last.

There are, nevertheless, two broad orientations that I want to take from experimental psychology into this account of satirical affect. The first is that emotions, far from being antithetical to thought as the Platonic and Cartesian mind-body dichotomy has it, are a crucial part of how we grasp ideas, impressions, and judgements. We do not think dispassionately, and certainly not when we are engaged in satirical cognition. This is not a novel proposition. It is at the heart, for example, of David Hume's (2011: 266) mid-eighteenth-century theory of passions (which I discuss in Section 3) where he notoriously holds that 'Reason is, and ought only to be the slave to the passions, and can never pretend to any other office than to obey them.' But the dream of reason has a habit of carrying us away, and its limits need to be relearnt regularly. The second

---

[8] See Plamper, 2015, especially chap. 3.

[9] See Pfaff and Gibbs, 1997; Simpson, 2003; Baumgartner and Morris, 2008; Lamarre, Landreville, and Beam, 2009; Refaie, 2009; Zekavat, 2017; this scholarship is further surveyed in Chen, Phiddian, and Stewart 2017.

orientation is that satire might, by the way it harnesses harsh emotions to more or less civil discourse, function in a culturally adaptive way. I mean this as a strong metaphor for the role satire can play in the cultural ecology of a tolerant and relatively free press, but I certainly do not claim the precise Darwinian sense of individual and group adaptation to maximum procreation and survival. Joseph Carroll (2004), Brian Boyd (2009), Denis Dutton (2009), and others have argued that art and narrative are adaptations that provide evolutionary benefit to humans. That may be so, but what I have to say does not depend on it. It depends on the weaker claim that the play of satire is part of the play of public emotions that permits peaceful and complex societies to flourish.

Satire is not exactly the opposable thumb of public discourse, but, sometimes paradoxically, it helps us avoid Hobbes's (1991: 88) notorious state of nature, 'such a warre as is of every man against every man'. As part of an active press, it provides an outlet for public passions and dispute short of actual violence. I argue these things in greater detail in the following sections, so I will put it here only schematically. The visceral emotions mobilised by satire are anger, or the aggressive desire to attack the object of criticism; disgust, or shocked recoil from the object; and contempt, or cool but harsh rising above the object. Why the satirical exercise of these powerfully negative emotions seems to be such a persistent element of relatively free presses (something nascent in the Scriblerians' time) is apparently paradoxical. How and why should anger, disgust, and contempt expressed in various modes of ridicule contribute to civil discourse? My hypothesis for this is a model of catharsis, whereby potentially disruptive public emotions and ideas can be exercised in public without recourse to violence or oppression.

Satire and Truth

But is not satire the mode of truth militant in a naughty world? Satirists often claim to tell the simple truth, and they very probably believe that is what they do. However, questions must follow: whose truth? what sort of truth? truth to what ends? They present their work as the defence of an underlying moral order that is being traduced, but they do not obviously (or rather, they obviously do not) play by ethical deliberative rules. Anyone who seeks to assess satires by a standard of detachment, balance, sympathy, or complexity of analysis will find little that makes the grade and will tend to the conclusion that satire should be deprecated, perhaps even suppressed, in the pursuit of a rational and sensitive public culture. Martha Nussbaum, whose work on anger I discuss in the next section, takes something like this line in a series of books (Nussbaum 2004, 2016, 2018). She argues powerfully that all interpersonal acts of shaming and expressions of disgust or anger fall short of the full mutual respect in which human relations should occur. There would be no satire in her *Republic* and she has a point. The central field of satire for the purposes of this study, political satire, is always a risk to the temperate quality of civil discourse. By a standard of rational and sympathetic truthfulness, the obvious public appetite for satire looks like a sociopolitical problem, perhaps akin to appetites for pornography and spectacular violence, which need to be contained by laws as well as cultural and commercial codes.

Even on the memorable occasions when satirists appear to have got the condition of their societies 'right' (e.g. Swift on colonised Ireland, Voltaire on *ancien régime* France, Orwell on twentieth-century totalitarianism), there is little that can be characterised as balance or respectful debate in the way they go about their business. Instead they caricature their targets' positions and physical appearance; they parody their discourses; they ridicule their sacred images. A satirical intervention will always 'other' its targets. So *Animal Farm* (1945) others the leaders of the Soviet revolution by presenting them as pigs and calling up the bestial baggage those animals carry in European literature. Orwell calls up a set of visceral identifications in the audience that is hard to characterise as good civic discursive behaviour. We may applaud him but, rightly, deplore racist depictions of Jews as rats or Africans as monkeys, and there is not much difference at a formal or technical level. Rather than give the meretricious *Der Sturmer* another run, consider the well-known and technically brilliant expression of White Australian xenophobia from the 1880 depicted in Figure 2.

No account of the public emotional effects of satire can dodge the fact that it is a mode that can be used to whip up dark and irrational passions. This cartoon stirs up feelings against what British Australians perceived as the 'Yellow Peril' of Chinese immigration to the young colonies. It now looks morally revolting, but it is an undoubtedly powerful image that only became infamous when the 'White Australia' policy came under concerted attack, after World War II. For decades it looked like plain common sense to most citizens of one of the more democratic countries of the world and may still appeal to some of my more extreme and paranoid compatriots. Should something this forceful be constrained by wise press regulation to limit error and offense?

Fortunately for those of us who enjoy satire and do not want to be locked up as moral perverts, there are at least two robust reasons not to institute such precautionary censorship. The first is that any system of censorship requires great faith in the guardians who choose the censors. History suggests that there is no reliable way of keeping them wise and sensible, or incorrupt. Moreover, the taboos shift. The unspeakable or undrawable changes over

Figure 2 Phil May, The Mongolian Octopus – His Grip on Australia. *The Bulletin*. Sydney, August 21, 1886.

time, so that the routine racism of the 1880s, now so offensive to us, passed without comment at a time when any publication of a realistic image of a naked body would have caused a riot. So censorship never works reliably or durably. The second, and perhaps more substantial reason, is a more broadly political one. Corrupt, complacent, or shameless rulers and regimes will not listen to reasonable critique and the public may well need shock therapy. Macalester Bell (2013: 273) writes of contempt (in some ways the hardest of the CAD emotions to defend) as an ethically apt response to the vices of *superbia*:

> It would be nice if no one ever evinced the vices of superiority, and in such a world contempt would not play the defensive role I've described. But we shouldn't respond to real and pressing threats in this world by pretending they don't exist, and that is why we should prefer an ethic of contempt to an anti-contempt ethic.
>
> Contempt can be a fitting, reasonable, prudent, and morally appropriate response to those who harbor *superbia*. It answers badbeing and is the best defense against the dangers posed by faults like arrogance, hypocrisy, and racism.

She was writing before the election of Donald Trump but is unlikely to have changed her mind on aptness. Sometimes the symbolic contempt of satire feels necessary, even if it appears to achieve little politically. A public life without public-shaming mechanisms would not only be a field day for the shameless. It would also be infuriating to all but saints of passive resistance.

This argument is as old as Juvenal's claim that in the Rome left by Domitian, *difficile est saturam non scibere* ('it is difficult not to write satire') (Iuvenalis, *Satire I*, l. 30, 1996: 46). It is as new as the North Korean government's hostile response to Seth Rogen and Evan Goldberg's mocking movie *The Interview* (2014). Louis-Philippe objected to being drawn as a pear by Honoré Daumier and *La Caricature* was suppressed (1835); Hitler had the pioneering newspaper cartoonist David Lowe on the Gestapo's list for arrest were the invasion of Britain to be successful (Kerr, 2000; Seymour-Ure, 2004). Such substantial despots deserve to be irritated, we feel. That people are compelled to compose satire and to respond to it is little more than a brute fact, however, and not a justification in itself. It leaves us with a number of questions: Where does the desire (or, according to Juvenal, compulsion) to vent satirically come from? What sort of sense of truthfulness does this obviously exorbitant venting appeal to in audiences who 'get' particular satires? Are there any systematic reasons why audiences might refuse to 'get' satires they have the cultural knowledge to understand? What is this 'getting' business anyway? We are a long way from having definitive answers to these questions. Rather, this study is an attempt to get the questions straight and then to get an exploration into the emotional drives and dynamics of satire underway.

The Emotional Publics of Satire

The creation myth of Aristophanes and Cleon that prefaces this Element is centrally about politics and public emotions, and it assumes that a major function of satires is to perform virtual political action, both for the authors and for publics who react.[10] These virtual political actions can have three broadly different sorts of political results: (1) the change in the world desired by the satirist; (2) a sensational reaction or response more or less at odds with the purpose of the satire, and (3) some consolation or even catharsis for those whose convictions are mobilised by the encounter with the satire. While satirists and their most committed publics tend to dream of the first sort of reaction vanishingly few examples of it occur in a neat and instrumental manner. Swift, through his *Drapier's Letters* (1724–5), did play a major role in stopping the imposition of Wood's copper coinage in Ireland; Tina Fey's caricature (2008–10) of

---

[10] The use of 'publics' rather than the more totalising 'the public' is derived from Warner, 2002.

vice-presidential candidate Sarah Palin probably did contribute to her demise as a serious political figure (Baumgartner, Morris, and Walth, 2012). No doubt there are more instances, but 'satires that got what they wanted' would be a slender volume. The US's full satirical-industrial complex currently seems in a helpless fury before President Trump's ascendancy, for example. A larger number of satirical interventions have gleaned a big but perverse impact, at odds with their apparent purpose. Daniel Defoe's *Shortest Way with the Dissenters* (1702) was initially understood as an attack on Nonconformist Protestants rather than the ironic defence of them it was intended to be. When the true intent was made public, Defoe was put in the pillory by the Anglican establishment for seditious irony (Novak, 2001). Similarly, the Danish newspaper *Jyllands-Posten* published a series of cartoons ridiculing Mohammed in 2005, expecting a reaction from Islamists, but it seems unlikely that their intention included death threats and police guards for the cartoonists or boycotts on Danish goods (Klausen, 2009). Once satirical provocation bites, there is little capacity to control where the public emotions will flow, and the political work a text might do becomes utterly unpredictable. The bulk of satire, however, fails to hit a prominent nerve, neither changing the world nor causing major controversy. A proposition central to this study is that such satire still does political work by allowing the catharsis of political emotions and ideas that cannot be fully assimilated to an ideally rational or respectful public debate. Even while aiming to offend, satires can help build functional tolerance of differing views.

There are clearly some regularities and paradoxes about the ways publics react to different satirical stimuli, and the rest of the Element will map some of them. The regularities broadly reflect the cultural business of testing and policing taboos on conduct in spheres as various as morality, politics, religion, aesthetics, and fashion. Individual contexts are endlessly various, but the social and discursive consequences of the public expression of satirical anger, disgust, and contempt have a lot in common across time and place.[11] So, where do these recognitions and emotions occur? Clearly the traditional formalist answer of 'in the text itself' is beside the point for affective analysis such as I propose. It is the audience who 'gets' a satire, but the category needs a bit of nuance as 'audience' is a bland and in some ways misleading term, for two reasons. First, especially for political satire, there is no single, uniform audience, but different groups with different levels of knowledge and prejudice. Second, satires claim a deeper level of civic engagement than is implicit in the notion of an audience, hailing

---

[11] There is, naturally, a huge body of scholarship on this in the psychology of emotions, trying to finesse a more nuanced position than Paul Ekman's universal emotions theory. One way into this work is Parrott, 2012, 2016.

them as citizens not just consumers of a cultural 'product'. Neither of these is a wrecking criticism of 'audience' as a term, but a different quality of engagement or passivity is implicated by a satirical fiction and a genre novel or a political cartoon and a comic strip. A more precise term for the quality of engagement implicated by satires is *public* as described by Michael Warner (2002). These publics are always plural and informal for Warner, and I take a term from Monique Scheer (2012) to describe how they are *mobilised* to think and feel in reaction to the satirical text.

Warner's publics and counterpublics are virtual creatures without institutional organisation. They occur as an informal gathering of common interest or feeling, which is how satires that are political in the broad sense find and mobilise their audiences. Satirical texts call a public into being, a public mobilised by an attitude towards certain objects of criticism. Thinking through satirical publics is part empirical research – literally, who might be being addressed and what might their concerns be? – and part a matter of interpretation inflected by reader-response approaches – how might this text have worked with the publics engaged? Any empirical audience reaction is extremely valuable information, but it is not the sole or sufficient goal of the process. A level of interpretation is always needed to think through the publics hailed and the emotions mobilised because a satirical text is not necessarily dead to further mobilisation. Many satires disappear in their moment and are of no more than cultural-archaeological interest thereafter, but some major texts still hail publics in the modern world. These tend to be the ones with a durable satirical fiction at their heart: for example Swift is often and validly turned to postcolonial purposes, and Pope is admired as a platform for charismatic gloom about falling standards. These satirical uses may be anachronistic to a strict historicist exploration, but that scholarly renunciation of current significance denies the recursive nature of understanding in humanities and the arts. Satires are designed to provoke, not to have determinate historical meanings. In a sense, they stop being satires when they lose the capacity to hail new publics and become *mere* historical data.

Questions of Scope

One thing that bedevils the study of satire is the need for thick context to explain the joke. Consequently, surveys of satire are difficult things to do well or make interesting. The aim of comprehensiveness almost inevitably takes a writer beyond her or his deep knowledge into a zone of thin acquaintance with the particular bite of the texts; even writers with encyclopaedic knowledge of many satirical contexts are unlikely to be blessed with readers who can genuinely follow them to all those places. Common sense suggests that the best account of satire would be the most comprehensive, but, at least in my view, common sense is wrong. The more extensive an account's coverage, the more bewildering or tedious it tends to become for actual, existing readers. So I frame my account as a specific history of public emotion, to focus on a single period and a limited group of writers. My choice is likely to be uncontroversial. The Scriblerian satirists of early-eighteenth-century Britain – Swift, Pope, and Gay – have been at the heart of literary debates about satire for hundreds of years. They also conveniently cover the three major literary media of prose, poetry, and drama. Only a discussion of the Roman poets Horace and Juvenal would be more classically conventional, and if my account of the negative emotions in satire can be made to work for the Scriblerians a lot of follow-on in literature and other media can be confidently expected. The burden of proof that I propose as a test is not that the following sections should demonstrate that *all* satire *must* be conceived in terms of the CAD triad of negative emotions, but rather that *a lot* of it *can* be, and that that realisation has significant heuristic potential.

It is inevitable that any account of satire will be inflected by the instances it treats as most central to the mode. Indeed, all attempts to generalise about cultural objects or patterns suffer from a version of this problem, because our data and their categories are always products of interpretation to a greater extent than those of the natural sciences. A theory of tragedy will always take Sophocles, or Corneille, or Shakespeare as more centrally typical, and this will have consequences for the theory. Accounts of comedy are conditioned by whether the central examples deployed lean towards aggressive or incongruous humour, comedy of situation or of repartee. Useful generalisation must start from recognition that there will always be bias, and that only bad faith can come from claims to transcend this condition. Perhaps a sufficiently scrupulous nominalism about the irreducibility of each cultural object or practice in its moment might escape the risk of bias, but it would encourage such resolutely agnostic analysis that it is better to accept that, for fruitful discussion of cultural types, there is no objective 'view from nowhere'. And so it is with this account of satire. As far as I can tell, it is partial for these reasons. I am by training a Swift scholar, and what he described as *saeva indignatio* on his tomb is for me a defining characteristic of the satirical (Phiddian, 1995, 2016). Even in the early eighteenth century, as Marshall (2013) rightly insists, satires were often gentler and more quizzical than Swift's. I attempt to take account of this in my reading of *Gulliver's Travels* in Section 4, where I explore the overlap between satire and comedy. However, this study is posited on a conviction that satire is a cultural practice derived primarily from indignation rather than amusement. My guiding assumption is that fierce wit is central to satire and that humour is something that often overlaps with satire rather than being a central constitutive element or umbrella concept for it. Laughter also attends satire very often, but not always, and it may have disparate qualities. Laughter at a child learning to walk is a gentler and more sympathetic thing than laughter at a corrupt politician caricatured as a pig – it marks the release of different emotions.

Another tilt in this account of satire is towards politics in the narrow sense of the word – towards the controversial and volatile political effects of satires, rather than towards broader cultural satire. A basic contention is that the CAD triad of negative emotions is integral (i.e. at least pervasive if not necessarily universal) to the affective operation of satirical discourse in various cultures, so I do not intend to exclude other social, aesthetic, or intellectual sub-modes. My core conception of the field is inflected by an appetite for political examples, so the main historical narrative pursued concerns the role satire plays in the development and practices of the freeish presses that characterise modern 'Western' democracies. My contention is that these conventions can be traced genealogically to eighteenth-century origins, particularly in British print culture, and that an appreciation of the necessary role of harsh and irrational public discourse can supplement more robust accounts of the early modern public sphere (Habermas, 1989; Lake and Pincus, 2006, 2007). It seems to me that public satire is an important if dark aspect of the enlightenment project and, for all its sometimes terrible indirections, a broadly civilising thing in the sense pioneered by the sociology of Norbert Elias.[12]

A high cultural tolerance for satire seems to be a necessary if not sufficient condition of robust conventions of freedom of expression. This is not only (or even often) because of any prophetic capacity of telling truth to power that satire may possess. Satirists often voice cranky, reductive, and moralising views, and there are very few to whom a sane polity would hand the reins of power. Satires, nevertheless, exercise a broadly cathartic capacity, a power to perform harsh public emotions in peaceful ways that are consoling to those (authors and their publics) rendered indignant by the way of the world. Just as Aristotelian catharsis fails to provide a completely satisfying theory of the emotional operation of tragedy, so satirical catharsis is only part of the story. It is a substantial part, however, especially if your focus is on a political

---

[12] For the very broad context of this assertion, see Elias, 1978; Pinker, 2011; Pagden, 2013.

ecology of free speech within stable political structures. This is a view of satire more as a liberal institution in a polity than as a radical mode of critique, although both characterisations can be accurate in different contexts. Authoritarian political cultures treat satire as sedition and suppress dissent. Freer ones allow for dissent's public performance, and satire can be a peculiarly satisfying way of doing this. Sometimes, of course, satires really do change minds, policies, and governments, but more often they console the disaffected as they rail against governments and leaders without going into the streets to overthrow them. Margaret Thatcher, George W. Bush, and John Howard are recent examples of democratic leaders who have withstood satire booms to rule for a long time. Donald Trump seems to be weathering another, though the 2020 election will influence history's judgment on that. Even if you share my view that they all led or lead poor governments, there is a liberal case to be made that we, the indignant, did better to enjoy the grim consolations of the satire rather than act on the desire to overthrow regimes by violent means. The emotional dynamics of satire provide an element of political stability, so satire seems a crucial element in actual if not ideal public spheres.

This Element aims to tell parts of the story of a group of historically formative satires' emotional dynamics in meaningful enough depth that readers can make a valid translation of the ideas to other contexts. The assumption is that there are regularities enough in satirical practices across time, space, and medium for this to be heuristically useful. A nested assumption within that, however, is that specificity of reference will always also matter. So the balance between general and specific that I seek to strike goes something like this: satire seems to exist in all cultures with something resembling a public sphere, but satire is also always for those in the know. The lines between insiders and outsiders used to be clearer in the age when politics' natural medium was print and institutionalised mass media. That seems to be changing in the digital world that has arrived with the new century and allows a proliferation of micro-publics much less defined by place or any need to broker a common (in)civility. If satire is a theatre for the exercise of harsh emotions, what happens when there is no capacity to limit who chooses to be the audience, where the conventions of giving and taking offense are disastrously unshared? In many countries during the age of print, satire played a role in the ecology of opposition paradoxically necessary for 'responsible government' and 'loyal opposition' to thrive. Whether it can continue to do so in the digital age is a matter for prophets, but scholarship in the history of emotions can provide an understanding of the dynamics of a liberal regime of public discourse that often worked well enough over a long period. That would be something.

2 Satire and the Contempt, Anger, Disgust (CAD) Triad of Emotions

Satire has generally been linked to, and often subsumed by, comedy and humour because the classic response to it is laughter. There is, indeed, a lot of overlap among these terms in common usage, which I address later in the Element. Here I focus on important aspects of the satirical mode that elicit unfunny feelings, precious little reconciliation, and harsh laughter at best. While it is certainly not a good idea to reduce one's sense of satire entirely to ridicule (Condren, 2012), there is a large tidal difference between satire, which tends to extravagant criticism in Timon's manner, and comedy, which tends towards the reconciling kindness and wisdom of Benedick: 'for man is a giddy thing, and this is my conclusion' (Shakespeare, V, iv, l. 112–13, 2008). A way of framing this tidal difference is to attend to the way satire mobilises (Scheer, 2012: 208–12) the 'moral', 'harsh', or 'negative' emotions, particularly the triad identified in neuroscience as CAD, for contempt, anger, and disgust.[13] I will not treat these psychologically defined emotions as empirical scientific bedrock – Paul Ekman's theory of universal basic emotions now commands little assent among neuropsychologists and has very plain inadequacies for historical and cultural analysis (Rottman, 2014; Plamper, 2015: 147–63; Parrott, 2016). The neuroscientific account of emotions is, however, sufficiently established to inform an exploration of the way public emotions circulate in satirical media. My proposition is that the way satires invite engagement in a public perfor-mance of these harsh emotions is a large and under-researched part of the compact made between satirists and their audiences. Many texts and images mix comedy and satire, often so that the shaming and critique integral to satire can slip past censors and the censorious as 'just a joke'. The satirical purpose in this mix will tend to be the mobilisation of contempt, anger, or disgust. While the presence of these emotions does not inevitably make a text or image satirical, it is a necessary if not sufficient ingredient of what distinguishes satirical humour from 'pure' comedy.

In the next section, I attend to the eighteenth century's sophisticated and in some ways better terminology of the passions, but here extend Joseph Carroll's observation that 'Together, anger, contempt, and disgust comprise the main emotional components of satire' (Carroll, 2004: 158). Maria Miceli and Cristiano Castelfranchi (2018: 206) succinctly delineate the family dynamics of hostile emotions: '[C]ontempt and disgust appear to be more closely related

---

[13] Rozin et al., 1999; Haidt, 2003, 2012; Gutierrez and Giner-Sorolla, 2007; Hutcherson and Gross, 2011; Russell, Piazza, and Giner-Sorolla, 2013; Ngai, 2014; Royzman et al., 2014; Plamper, 2015; Kollareth and Russell, 2017; Miceli and Castelfranchi, 2018, 2019.

to each other than to anger. Suffice to consider that whereas anger is qualified by attack action tendencies, contempt and disgust are both characterized by aversive responses.' Hanah Chapman and Adam Anderson (2012: 64–5) make a similar point and add a dimension of emotional cost relevant to satirical practices: 'Although anger may seem like a more natural response to norm violations than disgust, it is worth considering that anger is an approach-related, strongly activating emotion. Hence, it may represent a rather costly response to moral transgressions. By contrast, the withdrawal and avoidance motivation associated with disgust may offer a lower-cost strategy.' Crucial in both accounts are the basic moves: anger works by incitement while cold contempt and hot disgust are two modes (or moods) of aversion. In their classic form, the CAD emotions are behavioural responses to physical things such as threat and rotting food. However, they are also well recognised as broadly moral responses to human behaviour perceived as bad, low, or dangerous – the most material dimension for cultural analysis. It will, in due course, be appropriate to multiply terms to capture the full emotional range of satirical texts. Miceli and Castelfranchi (2018) include *resentment* and *indignation*; *bemusement* seems to me an important part of the palette that cannot be collapsed into the big three, while *disdain* may be covered by contempt, though it may not, exactly. I could go on. Precise words will eventually matter for contextually rich literary or historical analysis, but to see the broad outlines of the emotional terrain, the CAD triad is a useful heuristic for understanding the moralising tendencies of satirical verbal and visual rhetoric. In their seminal article, Rozin, Imada, and Haidt (1999) argue that these emotions police moral codes of autonomy (anger), divinity/purity (disgust), and community (contempt). While the typology of codes has been debated and modified in subsequent studies,[14] the existence of other-condemning emotions as public modes of critique is well established.

Benoît Dubreuil (2010: 35; see also 2015) frames the social implications of the punitive emotions thus: 'Shame, guilt, and embarrassment are usually held to underlie norm compliance, while anger, indignation, contempt, and disgust are largely associated with norm enforcement through the triggering of punishment behaviors towards norm violaters.' Satire fits here as a public mode of norm enforcement that deploys contempt, anger, and disgust in the hope of eliciting shame, guilt, and reformation in its targets. Satirists and their audiences hold this moral purpose to justify often harsh forms of stereotyping and othering. Whether these justifications hold up to scrutiny is much discussed among philosophers and cultural theorists of the emotions, and much of the rest of this

---

[14] See Gutierrez and Giner-Sorolla, 2007; Hutcherson and Gross, 2011; Royzman et al., 2014; Dastani and Pankov, 2017; Kollareth and Russell, 2017, 2019; Miceli and Castelfranchi, 2018, 2019.

section stages debates between the psychologists and the philosophers on how to value these emotions. Consequently, I seek here to define satiric emotional function in quite a structured way, by attending to philosophical and social-psychological accounts of each member of the CAD triad. I return to more historically grounded literary and cultural analysis in the next sections, but here for the sake of clarity I consciously run the risk inherent in neuroscientific approaches of synchronic universalism.

Disgust

Disgust is arguably the most distinctive element of the force of satire as a literary and artistic mode. Certainly it is not true that *all* mobilisations of disgust are dominantly satirical – consider Francis Bacon's (1954) 'Figure with Meat'. Its representation of a man between the halves of a bisected cow is like a parody in that it reworks Velasquez's portrait of Pope Innocent X, but to extrapolate a satirical argument as dominant in the painting (even a very broad one about the frailty of worldly glory) seems a stretch beside the grotesque psychological and corporeal force of the figure and the carcasses. Compared to anger and contempt, however, literary, dramatic, and artistic expressions of disgust tend to the satirical more often than to any other mode or genre. Anger (to use only ancient Western reference points) has been central to epic since Achilles in the *Iliad*, biblical narrative since Cain and Abel, tragedy since *Ajax*, and populist political rhetoric since Cleon. Contempt often appears as a social regulator of rank throughout the realist novel and comedy of manners, often without significant satirical charge. But if you are witnessing an aesthetically framed mobilisation of disgust, it is fair to say you are *probably* witnessing something with a major satirical dimension.

So, how is disgust understood as an emotion? Miceli and Castelfranchi (2018: 215) aptly summarise Rozin, Haidt, and McCauley's (2008) dominant synthesis of disgust as existing in four kinds:

> (a) core disgust – a reaction to stimuli pertaining to oral incorporation; in fact, disgust is primarily a rejection response to a 'revolting' food; (b) animal – nature disgust, evoked by stimuli reminding humans of their animal nature and vulnerability – such as corpses, filthiness, deformity, and body envelope violations; (c) interpersonal disgust, elicited by contact with undesirable (namely, unknown, diseased, unfortunate, or morally tainted) people; and (d) moral disgust, elicited by norm violations.

Clearly satirical mobilisation of disgust skews to the two latter, relatively social kinds, though grotesque eating and all sorts of corporeal (especially excremental) filth are persistent tropes in satire from Aristophanes, to Rabelais, to *South Park*. Indeed, the strongest impression left on me from a couple of happy days

Figure 3 *National Conveniences.* Etching. Photo by Fine Art Images / Heritage Images / Getty Images.

looking at hundreds of Gillray prints in the Yale Center for British Art is the quantity of literal and figurative defecation apparently performed by the leading public figures of the Napoleonic era. Gillray's (1796) excremental vision is particularly intense but far from isolated among satirists, as his reflection on national stereotypes shows (Figure 3).

One deep and intuitive cry of satirical texts is 'unclean!' It is fascinating to think that 'the neural and physiological correlates of moral disgust have been found to be similar to those of physical disgust, and different to those characterizing anger' (Miceli and Castelfranchi 2018: 218, quoting five indicative studies). It is thus highly probable (if beyond my academic capacity to adjudicate) that basic and moral disgust use very much the same wiring in the brain (Chapman and Anderson 2013). To liken a noisome politician to a rotting corpse or a pile of shit is thus no casual metaphor but a strong neural analogy of thought and arguably adaptive as a public emotion in the broadly evolutionary sense (Clark and Fessler, 2015). There is little difference in the mental processes of finding all these objects disgusting, and the cultural history of satire provides plenty of corroboration for this neuroscientifically strong hypothesis.[15]

In his influential account, William Miller (1997: 62) argues that 'Disgust, as embodied and visceral a passion as there is, comes to support a metaphysics of the physical in a way shame did not . . . Disgust is at home with the politics of pollution and purity.'[16] When it is a visceral and public passion, it drives satirical aversion through that politics of pollution and purity, in ways that can be moralistically coercive. This is controversial, with ethicists like Martha Nussbaum (2004) questioning whether such stigmatisation and shaming are ever a good idea (I address Nussbaum's reservations about the CAD emotions at greater length when I write of anger). Were people always willing to act rationally and sympathetically for the greater good, she would be right to counsel against ever using public stigma, but we act often on intuitive shortcuts, in public as in private life.[17] So disgust (and, by extension, satire) remains an inevitable part of political rhetoric and, as Michelle Mason (2010) argues in a discussion of shamelessness, a potentially apt one. Miller (1997: 197) is, nevertheless, correct to mark the moral failings of disgust, something particularly relevant to satirists who tend to overconfident moralising:

> Disgust, as we have supposed, is the moral sentiment that does the work of disapprobation for the vices of hypocrisy, cruelty, betrayal, unctuousness in all its forms: officiousness, fawning, and cringing servitude. It also polices those activities which I have described as the necessary evils of moral meniality and other moral matters of lesser moment. . . . Are these properly *moral* matters? Disgust has a vice; it is a moral sentiment of extraordinary inclusiveness and does more than register a simple aversion toward the objects of its focus. It degrades them in some moral way. As long as disgust is warring against cruelty and hypocrisy we are delighted to enlist it in our cause, but when it wars against the intrusively annoying or the deformed and

---

[15] See also Chapman and Anderson, 2012; Rottman, 2014; Kollareth and Russell, 2019.

[16] See also Menninghaus, 2003; Kelly, 2011; Korsmeyer, 2011; Herz, 2012; Eschenbaum and Correll, 2016; Lateiner and Spatharas, 2016.

[17] See Hume, 2008; Kahneman, 2011; Haidt 2012.

the ugly it may clash with other moral sentiments, like guilt and benevolence, that push us in another direction.

Satire similarly claims to be moral when it is often no more than moralising. To vary Miller slightly, as long as satire is warring against cruelty and hypocrisy we are delighted to enlist it in our cause. Swift (2018: 149-50) validly turns readers' stomachs in the *Modest Proposal* (1729) by enumerating cooking methods for babies: 'I have been assured by a very knowing *American* of my acquaintance in *London*, that a young healthy Child well Nursed is at a year Old, a most delicious, nourishing, and wholesome Food, whether *Stewed, Roasted, Baked,* or *Boyled*, and I make no doubt that it will equally serve in a *Fricasie*, or a *Ragoust*.' What, after all, is the difference between starving and actually eating the Irish but a few alimentary qualms? The risk of satirical overreach can be even graver for disgust-inducing satire than Miller fears, however. The long history of anti-Semitic caricature reached its apotheosis in *Der Stürmer*'s deliberately revolting images of Jews as unclean and polluting. Tempting though it is to say that these cartoons are so reprehensible as somehow not to be satire, I think we have to accept that they worked as satire in 1930s Germany, and not wilfully confine them to a separate and conveniently stigmatised category of propaganda. Satirical disgust has no reliable moral compass, and its force can sometimes serve appalling as well as apt goals. It is a pervasive activity in literary, visual, and performance cultures across time and space, but engaging satirical disgust is an ethically risky business. What presents as moral judgment and the rejection of pollution can easily fall victim to the vices of moralism.[18]

Contempt

Contempt is the second and cooler aversive emotion of satire. It is not always seen as an emotion separate from disgust because both signal intuitive avoidance of an object, but it is clearly a calmer, more social, and more lasting attitude than basic or animal-nature disgust. For a long time, it was much less researched than anger and disgust and may not be a natural kind of emotion because it lacks an intuitive facial expression (Barrett, 2006). As the dogmatic universalism of Ekman's basic emotions theory fades into history, however, the analysis of contempt as a psychosocial phenomenon is accelerating (Bell, 2013; Mason, 2018). A recent major article in *Behavioral and Brain Sciences* has sought to bridge the gap between its lack of experimentally definitive elements (unlike anger and disgust) and its functionally coherent features by calling it a sentiment

---

[18] See Taylor, 2012.

rather than a basic emotion or attitude (Gervais and Fessler, 2017). Gervais and Fessler (2017: 4) have drawn no fewer than twenty-six responses from scholars in a range of disciplines, and they identify eight features that a complete theory of contempt would need to explain:

1. Intentional, or about an object;
2. An enduring evaluation of a person, anchored by character attributions;
3. Follows from cues to another's low relational value, such as norm violations, incompetence, personal transgressions, and out-group position;
4. Entails loss of respect and status diminution;
5. Creates 'cold' indifference through diminished interest and muted prosocial emotions;
6. Associated with 'anger' and' disgust,' which are among the proximate causes, concomitants, and outcomes of 'contempt';
7. Can be expressed in many ways, including non-facial modalities;
8. Leads to intolerance, exclusion, and relationship dissolution.

Whether these features add up to a basic emotion or something else in brain science is still being debated, but there is clearly something going on here that makes sense as a social, group, or public emotion. Elements 1, 2, 4, and 8 seem particularly apposite for a lot of satire that downgrades its objects without being outraged or appalled by them. Miceli and Castefranci (2018: 223) summarise the different valences of contempt and disgust thus:

> Contempt involves an element of coldness; it seems to have a mixed valence, in that the feeling is both unpleasant and somehow pleasant; it is experienced exclusively towards human targets, and implies a sense of superiority over them, and pessimism about the possibility of their improvement. By contrast, disgust is typically hot and 'visceral', is utterly unpleasant, can be directed at a wide range of possible targets including inanimate objects and substances, and implies a sense of threat, and fear of the contaminating target.

Macalester Bell (2013: 46), in a rare book-length account of contempt, provides a summary definition of contempt that fits very well with a relatively calm, standards-maintaining sort of satire often exhibited by Jane Austen: 'contempt is a way of negatively and comparatively regarding or attending to someone who is presented as falling below the contemnor's baseline. This form of regard constitutes a withdrawal from the target and may motivate further withdrawal.' It is particularly apt as political satire when it answers the vices of *superbia* and Bell (2013: 8–9) summarises her positive valuation of the emotion thus:

> I will argue that contempt is an apt response to those who evince what I will call the 'vices of superiority.' These vices impair our personal and moral

relations, and contempt offers the best way of *answering* the damage wrought by these vices. While contempt may not seem to have a home amid the egalitarian values characteristic of contemporary moral theories, this shows the limitations of the standard interpretations of these theories. As moral agents, we must confront all kinds of immorality, and in some circumstances, we *ought* to harbor (and show) contempt.

She illustrates this normative claim with an uplifting story about a crowd contemptuously waving its shoes at Egyptian President Hosni Mubarak shortly before his fall from power in 2011. The subsequent political history of Egypt seems to suggest that, like satire, contempt can be apt without being politically effective in the long run. It seems unlikely that the shoe thrower envisaged the brief ascendancy of the Muslim Brotherhood (2011–13) and the subsequent ascent of the very Mubarak-like military government of Abdel Fattah el-Sisi (2014–present). Here again the moral slipperiness of satire emerges, where judgment is certainly forceful but not necessarily just, and the results are unpredictable.

Some of this can be seen in the way John Gay mobilises contempt in the first air of his *Beggar's Opera* (1728):

> Through all the Employments of Life
> Each Neighbour abuses his Brother;
> Whore and Rogue they call Husband and Wife:
> All Professions be-rogue one another:
> The Priest calls the Lawyer a Cheat,
> The Lawyer be-knaves the Divine:
> And the Statesman, because he's so great,
> Thinks his Trade as honest as mine.
>
> (Gay 2013: 5)

From these first notes, as I contend at greater length elsewhere (Phiddian 2017), contempt for human appetite and corruption is the key emotional thread of the opera. Peachum expects nothing better of the bar, the pulpit, and the throne than of himself, and his self-image is strikingly low. The inversion on 'honest', where the statesman is presented as aspiring to a thief-taker's status, is beyond sardonic. It downgrades 'the Great Man' Walpole with a contempt that does not even bother to make the details of satirical identification particularly precise.

So, contempt functions as a public or social emotion mobilised by satire. While relatively few will seek to defend Walpole, with his penchant for corruption in government, from contemptuous judgment, it is again important to point out that satirical contempt can also police reprehensible norms, as racist cartoons such as those enforcing Jim Crow stereotypes in the United States or European superiority over Aboriginal people in Australia attest. Satirical contempt used against the socially and politically weak can be particularly debilitating. If used to 'punch up' against powerful oppressors, it can be psychologically liberating.

Anger

Alexander Pope in his *ars satirica*, the *Epilogue to the Satires* (1738), gives the most superbly rousing call to satirical anger:

> O sacred weapon! Left for Truth's defence,
> Sole Dread of Folly, Vice, and Insolence!
> To all but Heav'n-directed hands deny'd,
> The Muse must give thee, but the God must guide.
> (Pope, *Epilogue to the Satires*, II, ll. 212–15, 1963)

This is the full Juvenalian rage for truth in its most histrionic form. It is pure satirical anger, an activating call to action, not a withdrawal from something contemptibly low or disgustingly noisome. It is also, Pope claims a few lines earlier, unmotivated by personal affront:

> Ask you what Provocation I have had?
> The strong Antipathy of Good to Bad.
> When Truth and Virtue an Affront endures,
> Th'Affront is mine, my friend, and should be yours.
> Mine, as a Foe profess'd to false Pretence,
> Who think a Coxcomb's Honour like his Sense;
> Mine as a Friend to ev'ry worthy mind;
> And mine as Man, who feel for all mankind.
> *(ll. 197–204)*

The claim to satirical impersonality is an enabling fiction rather than a biographical reality, for Pope and any other enraged satirist. Detached and objective animus is vanishingly rare. I have, however, deliberately changed the order of play in this section to start with a hyperbolic satirical evocation of the emotion rather than the psychological definition. Martha Nussbaum's reasoned disapprobation of the CAD emotions has ghosted the previous two sections and should now be confronted head-on. In *Anger and Forgiveness*, she mounts a powerful normative attack on all but something she calls 'transition anger', evident in the actions of Mahatma Gandhi, Martin Luther King (partly), and Nelson Mandela. In a subtle range of arguments (which I lack the space to give full justice to), she delineates the improperness and inutility of almost all other anger. Then she makes a normative claim that would incidentally ban the mobilisation of satirical anger:

[I]n a sane and not excessively anxious and status-focused person, anger's idea of retribution or payback is a brief dream or cloud, soon dispelled by saner thoughts of personal and social welfare. So anger (if we understand it to involve, internally, a wish for retributive suffering) quickly puts itself out of business, in that even the residual focus on the offender is soon seen as part of a set of projects for improving both offenders and society – and the emotion that has this goal is not so easy to see as anger. It looks more like compassionate hope. When anger does not put itself out of business in this way – and we all know that in a multitude of cases it does not – its persistence and power, I claim, owes much, even perhaps everything, to one of two pernicious errors: either to a fruitless focus on magical ideas of payback, or to an underlying obsession with relative status, which is the only thing that really makes sense of retaliation as ordinarily conceived. (Nussbaum 2016: 31)

I have quoted at such length because this seems to me a substantial moral argument against a core emotional justification of satire in general. On this account, satire would never, ultimately, be wise. It would always involve giving in to a self- and other-damaging pernicious error. Nussbaum's is, in many ways, an appealing case, but it rests on a utopian (or at least a severely stoic) assumption about human nature which she outlines earlier in a discussion of payback. She asserts that this can only be a form of 'magical thinking' to be discarded 'since we all want to make sense to ourselves and be rational' (Nussbaum, 2016: 29). Her sane person seems very rare in the passion-infused politics of the 2010s as it was in the 1730s. Moreover, her stance provides little capacity to resist leaders who are shameless enough not to want to make sense to themselves or be rational, a view that might reasonably be held of the current leaders of the United States, the Philippines, and North Korea, to name only some of the least debatable candidates. And I note that her paragons of apt transition anger – Martin Luther King, Mohandas Gandhi, and Nelson Mandela – all led movements very admirably that have been less well served by some of their successors, who have sometimes scurrilously lived off the moral capital of the founders.

As I am engaged in a pragmatic study of what satire actually does rather than what it should do, I do not necessarily need to address Nussbaum's argument and can merely quote her admission that 'in a multitude of cases' anger does not quickly put itself out of business, in satire or in life. However, I think Nussbaum is also too blithe about both the functional shamelessness of many who seek power and prestige,[19] and the capacity of humans to be universally consoled by progressive rationality and compassion. Jonathan Haidt (2012) in *The Righteous Mind* has made a contentious

---

[19] See Mason, 2010.

argument about the kinds of political affiliation that follow from the findings of moral psychology. While he overreaches in defining Democrat and Republican psychologies (the reasoning becomes circular), his case for the intuitive rather than rational nature of most actual moral judgments is empirically powerful. On Haidt's account, it is unwise to generalise about humans on the strength of surveying WEIRD (White, Educated, Industrialised, Rich, Democratic) subjects, and Nussbaum seems to assume such subjects acting on their best behaviour (Haidt, 2012: 95–111, following Henrich, Heine, and Norenzayan, 2010). A Swiftian may be inclined to see these ideally WEIRD judges of value as Houyhyhnms ill-equipped to deal with Yahoo tendencies in themselves and others except by blank stigmatisation. Haidt buttresses his anti-platonic view with Hume's profound challenge to the idea of a rational ethics in his proposition that reason is the slave to passion, not its master. One of the gathering achievements of the history of emotions is to demonstrate how broadly and deeply true Hume's sceptical view of reasoning is, and my account of the mobilisation of CAD emotions in satire strongly supports it.

To step back from the ancient contest between idealists and sceptics for a minute, however, let us outline an account of anger from cognitive psychology to match the accounts of disgust and contempt provided earlier. Owen Flanagan (2018: xvi) gives a convenient two-level summary. First are the three 'spheres of anger':

- *Personal:* Anger at family and friends.
- *Communal:* Anger in wider communal and commercial relations.
- *Political:* Anger at policies and institutions of government.

An understanding of satire will tend to focus on the communal and political spheres, but the personal cannot be discounted entirely. He then outlines seven subordinate 'types of anger':

- *Payback anger* where I intend to cause another physical or mental pain and suffering, and/or status harm, typically because he or she has caused me pain.
- *Pain-passing anger* where I intend to cause pain to another because I am in pain, but not pain that he or she caused.
- *Instrumental anger* where I am angry with you and express it with the aim to get you to behave, apologize, or fix things, but not mainly to cause you to suffer.
- *Recognition respect anger* where I do not wish for payback. I have been diminished and demand recognition respect as a way of restoring a sense of self-worth and as a signal that you are not the callous kind of person you just seemed to be.

- *Feigned, 'as if' anger* where I am not really angry or very angry in the inner phenomenal sense but use 'angry words' or threats to gain compliance.
- *Political or institutional anger* at social policies or laws or structures that are unfair, racist, sexist, or otherwise harmful or dehumanizing.
- *Impersonal anger* that expresses horror and fury at the heavens, nature, human evil, or folly. (Flanagan 2018: xvi)

How ethically apt these types of anger can be is open to debate; Flanagan suggests both that the two first and most visceral types are the most problematic morally and also that they are the most likely to inform the other five. His categories certainly provide a neat way of addressing false or mixed motives in satirical defences, including the popular contemporary one about a right to abuse being nested in a right to free speech. No party in the culture wars will admit to indulging in payback or pain-passing anger, of course, but the distinctions allow more dispassionate observers to pass better judgment on how grievously free speech has really been constrained or traduced. We are, however, again in ethically slippery territory for satire. Pope, in the lines quoted earlier, certainly claims pure and impersonal anger for himself or at least for his declamatory persona, and the rest of the *Epilogue to the Satires* runs further defences along these lines for instrumental and political/institutional anger. The *Dunciad* (1728–43) is a monument to recognition respect anger, and the *Rape of the Lock* (1712), though its sexual politics make this hard to experience nowadays, seems intended as a baroque exercise in feigned anger intended to produce compliance to a patriarchal sort of sense. But undercurrents of payback and pain-passing anger seem strong throughout his *oeuvre*, in characters like Atticus and Sporus in 'Epistle to Arbuthnot', Timon in 'Epistle to Burlington', and the scribblers of Grub Street throughout the *Dunciad*. They are no less likely to inform the defensiveness of Jon Stewart or P. J. O'Rourke today.

As Dubreuil (2015: 475) puts it: 'The emotion of anger has a long love–hate relationship with morality. On the one hand, anger often motivates us to sanction wrongdoing and uphold demanding moral standards. On the other hand, it can prompt aggression behaviors that are at odds with morality and even lead to moral disasters.' Anger is a dangerous emotion to mobilise, as can be seen when a satirical controversy goes wild. Salman Rushdie's *The Satanic Verses* (1988) achieved an unintended and unwelcome global notoriety following the Ayatollah Khomeini's *fatwa* in 1989, and the *Charlie Hebdo* cartoonists sparked a level of murderous rage no one should have to endure in 2015. Plots, police protection, and actual deaths are levels of escalation that satire might grandiloquently invite without being quite serious, but they do occur. Mostly, a satirist will be inviting an in-group to righteous anger at some vice or villain, and that is where it will end. But when it 'goes off' public anger can be a thoroughly costly emotion, as a standard psychological definition recognises:

> Unlike other negative emotions, which typically prompt avoidance behavior, anger tends to promote approach tendencies, in the form of attack although others have also noted an increase in avoidance as well. Consequently, anger results in higher energy expenditure, evidenced by greater autonomic arousal and behavioral activation and a greater willingness to take risks. These higher cost behaviors may be designed to prevent or terminate specific behaviors that are perceived as immediate threats to the self, and anger may also increase the willingness to incur costs in order to punish betrayal. (Hutcherson and Gross, 2011: 720, in-text references removed)[20]

Angry satire often aspires to perform public punishment – Pope talks about being proud of his arbitrary role, 'Yes, I am proud; I must be proud to see / Men not afraid of God, afraid of me: / Safe from the Bar, the Pulpit, and the throne, / Yet touch'd and sham'd by Ridicule alone' (*Epilogue to the Satires,* II, ll. 208–11, 1963). He attacks the knaves whom the system and their functional shamelessness would otherwise protect, he assures us, and mostly they just try to laugh it off. But occasionally those in power get angry enough to try suppression, or other moral vigilantes take the law into their own hands. Satire can mobilise public anger in (at least arguably) socially responsible ways, for example by stigmatising the enemy in time of war, but it can also further victimise victim groups. It is hot to handle.

Conclusion

Modern neuroscientific study of the CAD triad provides a useful if incipiently synchronic basis for understanding much of the emotional dynamics of satire. To cover the full affective range, we would no doubt need a few more emotion words like indignation, disdain, even disgruntlement, but contempt, anger, and disgust are enough to map most of the territory. The danger is that a cognitive approach might treat satire as if it were a universal phenomenon of sufficient formal distinctness to be scientifically testable. Rendered schematically, such a model of satirical affect could be almost a hydraulic representation of the harsh emotions, with measurable quanta of feeling welling up in different subjects exposed to different texts. That would be a bad direction to turn for a couple of reasons that I have outlined. First, satire is not so much a formal genre as a discursive mode that appears in many formal contexts. Much psychologically inflected humour scholarship addresses jokes as a universalizable experience because it is genuinely arguable that they have

---

[20] See also Tagar, Federico, and Halperin, 2011; Averill, 2012; Miceli and Castelfranchi, 2019.

Figure 4 Ron Tandberg, *The Age*. February 4, 1983; reproduced with permission.

the same deep structure across time and cultures. This will not work for satirical interventions in novels, mock documentaries, and the rest because they are structural shape-shifters. And the second reason they cannot be reduced to experimentally explorable phenomena to the same extent as jokes is that context matters in such a deeply and socially ingrained way – they are texts that hail subjects with specific cultural and subcultural markers. Figure 4 is my choice for the funniest satirical cartoon in modern Australian politics, but be warned: unless you have an excellent recollection of the circumstances of the 1983 Australian election, it will mean nothing to you.

If you are intrigued, you can find necessary background detail on the web,[21] but my intention here is to bemuse most readers, to show how 'getting' satire requires detailed contextual knowledge as well as fellow feeling with the satirist. It is also playfully artful in a way that separates it from the primary

---

[21] See Manning and Phiddian, 2013. I reassure foreign readers that very few Australians will remember enough to chuckle at this one.

emotional experience that is the object of neuropsychology. The play-frame of satirical expression always performs at least a minimal detachment both for satirists and their targets, and that makes reliable laboratory experiments into satire a quixotic dream.

The next section will take this CAD model for satire as a sort of kit into a political culture (or habitus), 'classic' for the mode of satire and distant from present ideological concerns – what I will call the *Craftsman* moment in 1720s–1730s Britain. There, openly, political satire and opposition thrived in historically unprecedented ways. Monique Scheer (2012; see also Plamper, 2015: 265–70) writes about emotional practices and how they are mobilised, named, communicated, and regulated, and I treat satire as just such a practice. That will involve taking the early modern language of the passions seriously as a subtle way of avoiding a crude emotional functionalism. It will also, through a focus on informal regulation of the passions in public discourse, permit some fresh thinking on the idea of a nascent public sphere once projected onto the period by Jürgen Habermas. How did satire, with its often extravagant and oppositional expression of intemperate feelings, contribute to the development of something messier but more historically consequential than the ideal public ratiocination imagined by Habermas? Is public space for the exercise of the moral emotions a necessary if not sufficient condition for the development of the freeish press? Swift, Pope, Gay, and Fielding had almost no major political victories in the long decades of the Sir Robert Walpole's domination, but I intend to argue that they generated a new resilience in the public emotions that served the print age very well.

3 The Passions, Satire, and Liberty of Expression in the *Craftsman* Moment

> It will, I know be said, by these libertine Stage-Players, that the *Satire* is *general*; and that it discovers a Consciousness of Guilt for any *particular Man* to apply it to *Himself.*
>
> (*Craftsman* 85, Feb 17, 1728)

Thus goes the *Craftsman*'s teasing description of the effect of Gay's *Beggar's Opera* and, with it, the open contract of satire in a functional public sphere (D'Anvers, 1731). Trevor Ross (2018: 232) argues of the press after 1695 that, 'Once licensing had lapsed ... parties seized on the press's power of dissemination and in so doing accorded legitimizing authority to public opinion.' Satirists were in the vanguard of this seizure. They claimed a social licence that goes something like this: 'My satire is moral and general, so if any particular public figures see themselves among the knaves and fools in my work, surely that is their problem, not mine.' It is a durable satirical fiction, because the people ridiculed must recognise themselves in the mirror Swift (2010) once described as 'a sort of glass wherein beholders do generally discover everybody's face but their own' in order to complain. If the complainants have access to effective methods of repression, then they can repress the insult totally, but if the satire enjoys some level of social or even legal licence, then they have to repudiate the criticism, ignore it, or make some pretence of enjoying the joke. No cultural change is as sudden or tidy as this on the ground, but it is broadly true that the early decades of the eighteenth century in Britain were a time of transition in press freedom, a hinge point between worlds where repression and toleration were dominant. While this nascent and lumpy toleration applied to many modes of expression in the rapidly expanding world of print, it is this section's contention that the famous satires of Swift, Pope, Gay, and Henry Fielding played a leading role in testing the liberty of political critique and extending its emotional range. The schematic version of what happened (which the section attempts to substantiate with greater historical detail) is that the satirists went out in public with spectacular and minimally shrouded attacks on Sir Robert Walpole and his government, then dared the Great Man to respond. His different responses say something about his capacity for emotional risk and make him a strange sort of hero in the narrative: he combatted opponents in print with his own propagandists and a suite of dirty tricks, but only theatrical satire drove him to direct censorship. Both responses had long consequences for the press and the stage.

The early eighteenth century in Britain saw the development of something resembling two-party government and a press culture where matters of public import could be debated with relative freedom and passion. It also saw a great age of satire, indeed a 'hypercanonical' one, according to a recent study (Greenberg 2018, p. 18). The indispensable trigger for this confluence was the parliamentary decision in 1695 to allow the lapse of prepublication licensing. This both expressed and unleashed an ideology of liberty of expression that developed during the century through literature, newspapers, and pamphlet wars as much as through philosophy (Ross, 2018; McBain, 2019). It is, of course, possible to see modes of broadly political debate in manuscript and print long before 1695 (Lake and Pincus, 2007, especially chaps. 2 to 9). Debate also continues about just how deliberate a decision the lapse of prepublication licensing was, or whether it was intended to serve what we would now see as a liberalising programme of political expression (Kemp, 2012). Still, these necessary qualifications do not negate the fact that recognisably political views circulated in print more widely after 1695 than before and developed a cultural licence that was shaped by the dynamics of those early decades. Satire certainly thrived in the court and manuscript-dominated milieu of the Restoration, but its later full emergence in print as a public mode of critique is a significantly different story (Love, 2004; Marshall, 2013). This occurred in the Queen Anne years with pamphlet wars and the advent of periodicals, most notably the *Tatler* and the *Spectator*. That period also had regular changes of the ministry and the balance of forces in the House of Commons that began to establish party-based parliamentary government. It was only after George I came over from Hanover, however, and a long period of single-party rule began, that satirists took on a role they still hold as the loudest part of the permanent opposition to machine politics.

I characterise these decades, which cover roughly the years from Swift's first *Drapier's Letter* (1724) to Pope's final *Dunciad* (1743), as the *Craftsman* moment to ensure that we see the period as a media phenomenon, not 'merely' a literary one. The advent of a wider, print-based discussion of public affairs has classically been represented by Jürgen Habermas (1989) as the development of a bourgeois public sphere of rational public discourse. You do not need to know much about how raucous late Stuart and early Hanoverian religio-political debate could be to recognise this as a philosopher's just-so story more than an empirical historical description. In the naïve form, Habermas imagines something rather like a seminar spontaneously appearing in coffeehouses. Some find the whole notion as unworkable (e.g. Condren, 2009), but my account aims instead to supplement its broad thrust with an understanding of the essential role of intemperate rhetoric for a properly functional and freeish public press. A less resolutely revisionist view is formulated by Mark Knights (2007: 252) wherein he makes room for irrationality in what was, nevertheless, a new forum in print for the formulation of public opinions: 'irrationality or the perceived degradation of critical-rational public debate was apparent at the very inception of the public sphere'. Satirical practices and the harsh emotions they mobilise play a spectacular and formative part in bringing irrationality inside the tent of public discourse. They stretch the emotional range of the publicly speakable beyond Habermas's coffeehouse ideal of dispassionate truth seeking and in so doing strengthen the development of two-party politics by giving public space to the indignant passions and frustrations of opposition. Thus the 1720s and 1730s are crucial to an understanding of satire's particular contribution to the program of liberty of expression and loyal opposition enunciated by Viscount Bolingbroke and *The Craftsman*.[22] Those decades see a long period of domination by one leader, Sir Robert Walpole, who generally chose (pragmatically more than as

---

[22] See Hammond, 1984; Varey, 1993; Gerrard, 1994; Lund, 2016; Hellmuth, 2018; McBain, 2019.

a matter of principle) to deflect, ignore, outpublish, or otherwise traduce his opponents instead of openly suppressing or imprisoning them.[23]

The history of emotions has considerable explanatory power here, particularly Monique Scheer's (2012: 210) adaptations of Bourdieu's idea of *habitus* to talk of an emotional space where 'Political activism also relies on the practice of negative feelings, as every good speaker knows.' As I have indicated briefly in the previous section and at greater length in individual articles, Pope's visionary anger, Swift's resounding disgust, and Gay's superb contempt are strikingly violent and compelling expressions of visceral emotion in the public space provided by publication (Phiddian, 2016, 2017; Phiddian and McBain, 2017). And yet, this violence was not treated, at least not formally, as sedition by the Walpole regime they targeted. Their accusations of corruption and malfeasance did not have to circulate as underground dissent, or be obscured by anything more than the formal deniability provided by transparent claims to fictionality. Such open, spectacular, and sustained dissent to a current regime is a cornerstone of modern liberal notions of freedom of expression, but it was almost unprecedented before early eighteenth-century Britain. Moreover, Walpole's functional shamelessness is, on this reading, constitutionally productive for the practices of the fifth estate, as the major Scriblerian satires were among the contemporary *causes célèbres* in pushing the limits of criticism. Ashley Marshall (2013) has demonstrated that the canonical satires of Swift, Pope, and Gay were far from typical in the period, but for my purposes their prominence at the leading edge of outrage and outrageousness is more important than their closeness to median satirical practice. I am not seeking to 'defin[e] new archives and map ... new fields of intermedial movement', which Eugenia Zurosky praises Marshall, Simon Dickie, and others for in a recent review article (Zuroski, 2019; see also Dickie, 2011). I am trying instead, through attention to hypercanonical texts in a formative period, to map relatively durable emotional and political elements of satire.[24]

Ridicule, Good Humour, and Enslaving Passions

I am proposing political, quasi-constitutional consequences of satires as the emotional outliers of an ascendant ideology of liberty of expression. To do this, I need to build a bridge from the twenty-first-century neuropsychological language of the emotions to the eighteenth-century framework for discussing

---

[23] The lack of much current attention to Walpole is a bit of a mystery. There is a journalistic biography (Pearce, 2007), but Plumb's incomplete work from the 1950s remains central, and Taylor's long *Oxford Dictionary of National Biography* article is probably the main current resource (Plumb 1956, 1960; Taylor 2004).

[24] For an approach that mixes genre regularities with historical particularities, see Greenberg, 2018.

public and private feeling, the passions. Contempt, anger, and disgust were all words the Scriblerians used freely for modes of indignation, but they situated them differently from current perspectives – less scientifically, certainly, but in some ways more effectively for encompassing the whole social and affective picture of group emotions. The passions can provide a supplement and to some extent an antidote to the instrumentalism of current emotions research, which can be seen at its reductive universalist worst in Ekman's basic emotions theory of transcultural facial expressions (Plamper, 2015: 147–63). Much of what is valuable for an understanding of satire in Haidt's (2012) attempt to diagnose party political allegiance by reference to anchoring assumptions in the brain comes through his attention to the eighteenth century's largest philosophical claim for the passions. He quotes the famous formulation from David Hume's *Treatise of Human Nature*, 'Reason is, and ought only to be the slave of the passions, and can never pretend to any other office than to serve and obey them' (Hume, 2011: 266). This is a blunt explanation for why satirical rhetoric, though framed as rational and emotive persuasion, seldom actually shifts its audience's views, though it can be a powerful aid to confirmation bias. Even more apposite, in Hume's *An Enquiry Concerning Human Understanding*: 'Ambition, avarice, self-love, vanity, friendship, generosity, public spirit; these passions, mixed in various degrees, and distributed through society, have been, from the beginning of the world, and still are, the source of all the actions and enterprizes, which have ever been observed among mankind' (Hume, 8.7, 2008: 60). The list of passions covers much of the emotional content of satire, and Hume's (probably ironic) grandiloquence can be read as mimicking the mode. As I have argued elsewhere, Hume seems to be a satirist *manqué* and certainly has a satirist's appreciation for the emotional force of rhetoric, in the mind and on the ear (Phiddian, 2011).

Hume's passions have social and even intellectual agency beyond the narrow behavioural compass of neuroscience. They speak through individuals and groups to human purposes and conflicted loyalties. The passions play a crucial role in 'actions and enterprizes' as well as states of mind, and Aleksondra Hultquist (2017: 73) concludes her more general account thus:

> As a system of emotional knowledge, the passions were implicated in the physiology, psychology and social constructs of the [early modern] period. They were central to understanding how and why people as individuals and groups responded to the events in the way they did. They were the basis of action and they explained what we might call personalities. The passions are not synonymous with the twenty-first-century concept of the emotions; instead, they are indicative of entire systems of feeling in

the early modern world that structured both individual and collective identities and actions.

A holistic view of the passions allows us to see Scriblerian satire as contributing to a system of feeling which develops in the technological and political circumstances of the relatively free publication of journals and other forms of literature in the early Hanoverian period. This public expression of indignant passions permits the social circulation of anger, contempt, and disgust in oppositional ways that were not automatically repressed as sedition. In broad historical terms, this is different from all but the most unruly moments of the seventeenth century. Moreover, something like this transition seems generally to occur in places with freeish presses (no press is fully free), and satire then operates very differently from its function in authoritarian societies. There the authorities tend to repress satire, make it speak in deep disguise, or use it for propaganda purposes.

In the *Craftsman* moment, by a confluence of circumstances, a pragmatic toleration of satire permits a transition from a Hobbesian towards a Shaftesburyian view of the function of humour and ridicule. Hobbes (1991: 43) defines laughter essentially as rank-defining scorn in his famous phrase from *Leviathan* (1651) 'Sudden Glory, ... the apprehension of some deformed thing in another, by comparison whereof they suddenly applaud themselves.' This fits the harsh Juvenalian satire of the early seventeenth century and the Civil War and is clearly a mobilisation of disgust and contempt in my model, but it is hard to see it serving a functional tolerance of broad political expression. By contrast, half a century later, the Third Earl of Shaftesbury (1963: 9) took a benign view of wit and ridicule as socially and intellectually productive, first in *A Letter Concerning Enthusiasm* (1708):

> If the knowing well how to expose an infirmity or vice were a sufficient security for the virtue which is contrary, how excellent an age might we be presumed to live in! Never was there in our nation a time known when folly and extravagance of every kind were more sharply inspected or more wittily ridiculed.

Wit here is allied to ridicule as a sharp sort of inspection rather than a visceral rejection, and it is soon given a civilly productive function in *Sensus Communis; An Essay on the Freedom of Wit and Humour* (1709):

> [W]it will mend upon our hands, and humour will refine itself, if we take care not to tamper with it, and bring it under constraint, by severe usage and rigorous prescriptions. All politeness is owing to liberty. We polish one another, and rub off our corners and rough sides by a sort of amicable collision. (Shaftesbury, 1963: 46)

In Shaftesbury's playful philosophy, politeness leads by polyptoton to polish and performs a high level of benign whiggish optimism that trusts in the power of liberty of expression. This is an ideal image of amicable collision (something like Habermas's public sphere) rather than an accurate representation of actual pamphlet wars, but it is compatible with Pope's equally high sense of satire as a 'sacred weapon' put into 'Heav'n directed hands' (*Epilogue to the Satires*, II, ll. 212–14, 1963). Both views, from either side of the Whig and Tory divide, treat wit and ridicule as a public process of moral self-regulation and as a vent for proper indignation.

Few went so far as Shaftesbury to define ridicule as public virtue, but a lumpy ideology of press liberty built up after the 'Glorious' Revolution and in the early decades of the eighteenth century (see Lund, 2016; Hellmuth, 2018; McBain, 2019). Much of this occurred in the undefended territory between what we would now separate as literature and politics. The poetic imitation of Horace, pursued by Pope and his many opponents (and analysed by too many critics to number here), opens a space for speaking unpleasant truth to power in a formally ambiguous but broadly understood manner. Similarly, André Dacier (Aristotle, 1705) could preface his translation of Aristotle's *Art of Poetry* with a model of tragic catharsis which governs the passions so as to achieve 'the only Aim of true Politicks', which 'is to procure to the People Virtue, Peace and Pleasure'.[25] A general argument about print culture making room for impassioned debate and ridicule was also driven particularly by the major satires of the age, as we will see next.

Satire and the Public Sphere for Contempt Anger and Disgust

The major satirical works of the 1720s and 1730s mapped and influenced an expansion of the political and emotional range of public opinion. They brought indignant passions that map closely to the CAD triad to the new oppositional politics of the period. As Ross (2018: 21) argues, 'the elites expected the people to perform no more than a supporting role in politics, yet the increasingly public nature of their contests implicitly accorded a measure of recognition to an idea of the public as a deliberative body that was independent of the state.' This is a historically supple reformulation of the public sphere narrative which relies on Michael Warner's (2002; see also Greenberg, 2018) account of how there is never a monoglot public, but many publics and counterpublics hailed into being by different sorts of address and discourse. Ross (2018: 21) states that the 'latter half of Walpole's regime [was] a watershed', for the hailing of a public as

---

[25] Aristotle, 1705; there are editions from 1705, 1709, and 1714 in *Eighteenth Century Collections Online*.

citizens more than as subjects; then he gives an account of how developments in the laws of licensing, copyright, defamation, and seditious libel shaped liberty of expression throughout the eighteenth century. He concedes Andrew Bricker's (2014: 915) point on the legal inutility of the satirical convention of blanking out proper names: 'we need to keep in mind that gutted names continued largely to be used not for legal reasons – they served no legally recognized function – but for vaguely ethical ones.' Then he notes a wider attitudinal licence whereby 'Satirists may have been emboldened to risk defamation claims because harmfulness of this force was becoming so doubtful and contingent on circumstance that mere insults no longer seemed actionable' (Ross, 2018: 278). The idea that simply avoiding the names of the great in satires would give you legal protection had always been a fantasy, but its prevalence shows that a less formal social licence of ridicule became, in Shaftesbury's phrase, *'sensus communis'*, or common sense. We can see this play with name-calling at its exuberant best in Pope's *Epilogue to the Satires*:

> *Friend* Yet none but you by Name the guilty lash;
> E'en Guthry saves half Newgate by a Dash.
> Spare then the Person, and expose the Vice.
> *Pope* How, Sir! not damn the Sharper, but the Dice?
> Come on then Satire! Gen'ral, unconfin'd,
> Spread thy broad wing, and sowze on all the kind.
> Ye Statesmen, Priests, of one Religion all!
> Ye Tradesman vile, in Army, Court, or Hall!
> Ye Rev'rend Atheists. *F.* Scandal! Name them, Who?
> *P.* Why that's the thing you bid me not to do.
> Who starv'd a Sister, who foreswore a Debt,
> I never nam'd; the Town's enquiring yet.
> The pois'ning Dame – *F.* You mean – *P.* I don't. *F.* You
>   do.
> *P.* See, now I keep the Secret, and not you!
> The bribing Statesman – *F.* Hold, too high you go.
> *P.* The brib'd Elector – *F.* There you stoop too low.
> *P.* I fain would please you, if I knew with what;
> Tell me, which Knave is lawful Game, which not?
>   (*Epilogue* II, ll. 10–27, 1963)

Pope is mobilising a public anger here in a glittering dialogue of couplets that explode the good, or at least prudential, intentions of his interlocutor. We all want to know who the 'pois'ning Dame' is, as long as we do not have to be held responsible for prurience. Consequently, there is no maintaining face and decorum with the knaves and fools who, according to the *Craftsman*'s long campaign, were corrupting the nation and its institutions. He is also playing outraged and outrageous peekaboo with Walpole when he hails the 'bribing Statesman' in line 24, only to have his Friend seem to talk him back from the ledge. Feeding an appetite for scandal becomes a public service, it seems, when the knaves have taken over.

So sanguine or impudent an attitude was vanishingly scarce in public before the 1720s, and a brief account of the reception of the major satires illustrates how the path was negotiated at least in part through satire. Basically, they started allusive and grew more explicit as more was passively tolerated by a failure to prosecute. The Scriblerian satires can in this light be treated as a project in the mobilisation and catharsis of what Swift called savage indignation and I would also call contempt, anger, and disgust. This project runs parallel to the *Craftsman*'s opposition to Walpole's regime and starts with the thoroughly fictional and often obliquely coded political critique of *Gulliver's Travels* (1726), which I - discuss in detail in the next section. It then moves through Pope's proxy war on propagandist writers in the first *Dunciad* (1727), to the more direct attack on immoral 'Greatness' in Gay's *Beggar's Opera* (1728) and *Polly* (1729). At this point, Walpole showed a greater appetite for outright suppression of satire in the theatre than in print, by keeping *Polly* from the stage. The satirical plays of Henry Fielding and others flourished in the 1730s only until the Stage Licensing Act of 1737. Along with a restriction of performance to two highly commercial and easily supervised theatres, the act stopped satirical performance and turned British drama down a different, more politically disciplined path than printed forms of literature (Kinservik, 2002). Meanwhile, Swift had largely retired from public controversy, but Pope wrote with growing impunity in an almost direct challenge to the king in his 'vile encomium' that contrasted George II with the Emperor Augustus in his 'To Augustus' (1737) and his even blunter *Epilogue to the Satires* (1738). Gulliver announced the war of words (8 August 1726) some months before Bolingbroke's *Craftsman* began its twenty-five-year run (Varey, 1993: 58; Swift, 2012). By 1742, when Walpole finally resigned as first minister, the dual ideas of press opposition to the ministry and politicians needing to be seen to take a joke were firmly enough established to survive in Britain, except in wartime, until today.

It is important to realise that Walpole might have introduced a more repressive licensing of the press, of a kind that existed almost everywhere else in Europe at the time. He seems to have considered and rejected a reintroduction of press licensing in the early 1720s and also went as far as using the Post Office to frustrate the circulation of opposition journals 'especially at times of political tension' (Hellmuth 2018: 160). The possibility of punishment for libel and sedition never disappeared and was applied more harshly away from the centre of power in London; Swift's printer for the *Drapier's Letters*, John Harding, died in 1725 while imprisoned in Dublin for his part (Pollard, 2000: 274–5; Ehrenpreis, 1962–83: vol. 3, 308). In the public forum opened up by the existence of periodicals undisciplined by prepublication censorship, and unevenly policed by libel and sedition laws, Walpole generally managed rather than ruled. As Bricker (2014) makes clear, the laws would have permitted him to be more heavy handed.

Gay's Contempt for Walpole and His Works

FIRST PLAYER.	But how can you hinder malicious applications?
POET.	Let those who answer for 'em who make 'em. I aim at no particular persons, my strokes are at vice in general: but if any men particularly vicious are hurt, I make no apology, but leave 'em to the cure of their flatterers.

(*Polly*, 1729)

Provocation from theatrical satire brought out the most severe formal strictures from the Walpole regime, first with Gay's ballad operas in 1728–9 then with Henry Fielding and the establishment of a Licensing Act for the stage in 1737. A pragmatic distinction developed between satire in print, which was to be harried and blocked in various ways but broadly allowed to exist, and dramatic satire, which required complete control. Walpole's intuition instituted a durable state of affairs in the Anglophone regimes for the next couple of centuries: print satire has, by-and-large, been liable only to post-publication forms of censure while dramatic performance was closely vetted before going public. The assumption that private reading is somehow politically and emotionally safer than being in an audience subject to ambiguities of performance and group emotions is only now collapsing. As the age of print and mass media gives way to digital media's novel patterns of isolation and togetherness, we have new ways of forming virtual mobs that are yet to be 'civilised' by law or convention. The medium conditions not only the message but also how it is experienced emotionally.

I have written at greater length on what I take to be the politico-cultural phenomenon that ran from January 1728, when the *Beggar's Opera* was first staged, and the end of 1729, by which time the controversy over the suppression and print publication of *Polly* had largely died down (Phiddian, 2017). Here I want to reprise the *Beggar's Opera*'s mobilisation of an intense but detached contempt, and Walpole's public performance of good humour in response to it.

The *Beggar's Opera* ends with a calculated metatheatrical bathos which is hard to read as a call to insurrection. Instead, it seems calculated to mobilise a high level of cynical detachment in the audience and contempt for the corrupt ways of the world. Macheath is taken by the authorities and claimed as husband by Polly, Lucy, and (as he says) 'What – four Wives more! – This is too much' (Gay, 2013: 68). He gives himself over to the Sheriff's officers for execution, but the Player and the Beggar (whom we have not seen since the beginning of the play) intervene:

PLAYER.   But, honest Friend, I hope you don't intend that *Macheath* shall be really executed.

BEGGAR.   Most certainly, Sir. – To make the Piece perfect, I was for doing strict poetical Justice. – *Macheath* is to be hang'd; and for the other Personages of the Drama, the Audience must have suppos'd they were either hang'd or transported.

PLAYER.   Why then, Friend, this is a down-right deep Tragedy. The Catastrophe is manifestly wrong, for the Opera must end happily.

BEGGAR.   Your Objection, Sir, is very just; and is easily remov'd. For you must allow, that in this kind of Drama, 'tis no matter how absurdly things are brought about. – So – you Rabble there – run and cry a Reprieve – let the Prisoner be brought back to his Wives in Triumph.

PLAYER.   All this we must do, to comply with the Taste of the Town. (Gay, 2013: 68–9)

The emphatic framing and manipulation of the plot deflates the drama and emotion, in almost an inverted image of Pope's mighty incitement to anger discussed later. It contemptuously challenges the audience/Rabble to want real satirical justice rather than the sentimental wish fulfilment of comedy. In this play, "'tis no matter how absurdly things are brought about,' and, by extension, thus goes the political world that ghosts the criminal underworld throughout. Walpole is not mentioned and he is not easily equated with any one character in the *Opera*. But he is there behind the scenes, the machine politician unconcerned by how absurdly things are brought about. He even sought to own the criticism and try to turn it to popular advantage. In his relatively unscholarly biography, Edward Pearce's (2007: 338) background as a political journalist helps him get this bit right:

> *The Beggar's Opera* does not concentrate all its delectable invention upon a single Walpole character. Gay had ironies to spare. Peachum, the main Walpole figure, recurringly called 'The Great Man', is thief-taker, fence and impresario of larceny. He is disclosed early in the play reading through a personnel manager's checklist of subcontracting robbers and thieves, concluding it on the climax of 'Robin of Bagshot alias Gorgon, alias Bluff Bob, alias Carbuncle, alias Bob Booty'. Robin of Bagshot is another allusion to the

Chief Executive of the Robinocracy, but so, arguably, is Macheath. No one seems to have worried about duplication.

Walpole spent a lot of money on pro-government propaganda, and there is plenty of evidence that he took no pleasure in being ridiculed.[26] But he did not immediately crack down on *The Beggar's Opera* and did not wish to be seen attacking it. The story goes that he bought a box for the second night of the play and clapped ostentatiously, encoring the song 'That levelled at me' to show the functional shamelessness in the face of satirical contempt that we now recognise as essential to any long-term politician beholden to public opinion. Gay's most authoritative biographer, David Nokes, cannot find definitive proof that the event occurred but is inclined to believe it: 'Sadly, there is no reliable evidence to confirm this anecdote, though it has the ring of authenticity as an example of "Bluff Bob's" own skills in political theatre' (Nokes 1995: 435). Walpole's supporter, Lord Hervey, gives the sort of contemporary evidence that lets us share Nokes's belief in good conscience: 'Even those who were most glanced at [in *Beggar's Opera*] in the satire had prudence enough to disguise their resentment by chiming in with the universal applause with which it was performed'. The one *most* glanced at can hardly be anyone but Walpole, and chiming in with applause gives the fable some further support. Hervey (1855: 120–1) then goes on to say that Walpole got Grafton to suppress *Polly* 'rather than suffer himself to be produced for thirty nights together upon the stage in the person of a highwayman'. Even if 'merely' a legend, the story shows a new relationship between power and the political emotions, a performance of good humour that deflects rather than silences satirical contempt aimed at corruption. It continues to be a regular trope of modern politics.

Pope's Provoking Anger in the *Epilogue to the Satires*

Down, Down, proud Satire! Tho' a Realm be spoil'd,
Arraign no mightier Thief than wretched *Wild*.

(*Epilogue*, II, ll. 38–9, 1963)

Walpole's one-off suppression of *Polly* was followed, after some years of increased satirical provocation on the stage led by Henry Fielding and others, by the Licensing Act of 1737 (royal assent June 21) (Swindells, 2014: 112). It had major consequences, reducing the capacity of theatre to engage in public matters until well into the twentieth century. Kinservik (2002) points out that the theatre became self-censoring under the pressure of limited venues and fear of the lord chamberlain. Among the more immediate consequences was an outcry

---

[26] See particularly chaps. 1, 2, 7, 8 in Black, 1984.

in print in which Alexander Pope, despite his claim in the *Epistle to Arbuthnot* (1735) that 'The Play'rs and I are, luckily, no Friends' (l. 60), played a prominent part. Jennifer Snead (2010) shows the *Dunciad* of 1743 to be a response to the act. The *Epilogue to the Satires* forms an even more immediate and angry response to an increasingly repressive regime. Dialogue I was published on 16 May 1738 and Dialogue II on 18 July at a time when he was also secretly printing and circulating Bolingbroke's *Idea of a Patriot King* (Erskine-Hill, 1981: 138; Mack, 1985: 709). I described earlier how anger is 'qualified by attack action tendencies' (Miceli and Castelfranchi, 2018: 206), and that is true of Pope's militant spirit in this pair of dialogues. He was also intensely personal in his attacks, with a minimum of allegorical deflection. The epigraph to this subsection pretends that attacking Jonathan Wild (hanged in 1725) is somehow impotent, but in the stablest of ironies, 'everyone' knew that Wild was a satirical analogue for Walpole. In the wake of the extension of censorship to the theatre, Pope almost directly challenges the prime minister to extend control over print as well or accept the validity of the satirical criticism.

The operatic, even apocalyptic, ridicule of the final lines of Dialogue I would have been unthinkable in print in the seventeenth century, or perhaps even at the start of the 1720s. There is almost no semblance of fiction here, just barely contained outrage:

> See thronging Millions to the Pagod run,
> And offer Country, Parent, Wife, or Son!
> Hear the black Trumpet thro' the Land proclaim,
> That NOT TO BE CORRUPTED IS THE SHAME.
> In Soldier, Churchman, Patriot, man in Pow'r,
> 'Tis Av'rice all, Ambition is no more!
> See, all our Nobles begging to be Slaves!
> See, all our Fools aspiring to be Knaves!
>
> *(Epilogue I, ll. 157–64; 1963)*

All the formal institutions of the nation are arraigned as corrupt, brought to account only by the charismatic power of satire and the savage wit in the grim idea of all the fools aspiring to be knaves (still a fair characterisation of financial markets on a bad day). Then Pope (I, ll. 171–2) modulates the emotional force by invoking a much calmer (and aversive) emotional response in the final couplet of the Dialogue, 'Yet may this Verse (if such a Verse remain) / Show, there was one who held it [Villainy] in disdain.' The overriding affect here is oppositional passion, of public attack on the current regime and its corruption. Pope's towering political anger in the public sphere received no direct response from Walpole, despite the fact that it would have been easy enough to demonstrate that he is the 'man in Pow'r' attacked here, and the poems directly criticise his recent marriage to long-time mistress Molly Skerrit. If, as seems likely, Pope was writing with the Licensing Act in mind, he seems determined to test Walpole's assumption that the mob emotions potentially available in theatres were more to be feared than individual ones elicited by private reading.

Shaftesbury's (1963: 9) benign view of 'folly and extravagance' being 'sharply inspected [and] wittily ridiculed' waxes violent in Pope's hands. This is also far more explicitly personal than Swift in *Gulliver* a little more than a decade earlier, as we see in the next section. Pope might easily enough have been prosecuted for seditious libel had Walpole been willing to make a cause of it, but he did not. The modern liberal convention that you make a fool of yourself by complaining about satirical attack was not yet robust, but Walpole, in his functional shamelessness, seems to have honoured it in embryo. Perhaps it was some Old Whig commitment to freedom of the press. More probably it was just pragmatism. We need a new and scholarly biography of the 'Great Man' to seriously address those questions. Nevertheless, within the play-frame of satirical writing, the Scriblerians had mobilised the indignant passions of contempt, anger, and disgust for a public that opposed the government but did not see themselves as rebels. In the next section, on *Gulliver*, I argue that this performance of emotion, though it did little to undermine the Walpole regime and its patterns of patronage, allowed a degree of political catharsis essential to any actual, existing public sphere. Maynard Mack (1985: 726) suggests something like this for the satire in the Horatian poems and particularly the *Epilogue*: 'The very structure of these poems . . . may have possessed for Pope a psychic as well as poetic utility affording him a theatre for his own ambivalent feelings about the society that had bred him and excluded him, caressed him and hurt him.' A loyal opposition should, of course, patriotically serve the nation by proposing sound and sober alternatives to government plans. But they need sometimes to be able to vent their spleen.

4 *Gulliver's Travels* – 'Wit, Confederated with Truth'

Samuel Johnson is generally considered an enemy to Swift's critical reputation, not least because of the grand dismissal of *Gulliver* recorded by Boswell (2014: 319): 'When once you have thought of big men and little men, it is very easy to do all the rest.' However, when being more deliberate (and less competitive, perhaps) in his 'Life of Swift' (1780), he comes up with a judgment germane to the concerns of this study:

> When Swift is considered as an author, it is just to estimate his powers by their effects. In the reign of Queen Anne he turned the stream of popularity against the Whigs, and must be confessed to have dictated for a time the political

opinions of the English nation. In the succeeding reign he delivered Ireland from plunder and oppression; and shewed that wit, confederated with truth, had such force as authority was unable to resist. (Johnson, Vol. 3, 2014: 208)

Johnson sees Swift as an influential political writer rather than as the sort of poet-philosopher ironically hymned in chapter 10 of *Rasselas* (1759). Writing far closer to Swift's day than to ours, he judges him by political impact rather than as what we would call (with a certain post-Romantic aura) literature. In terms of its effects as political satire, Johnson was almost certainly reading Swift's achievement less anachronistically than twenty-first-century readers in literature departments tend to do. Indeed, he sees Swift's impact on public opinion, in England and then in Ireland, as the point of his work, and as historically significant.

We now tend to assume that 'wit, confederated with truth, has such force as authority was unable to resist' is an eternal truth, and Johnson's ever-emphatic manner frames it as one. Even in 1780, however, he was being performative rather than simply descriptive in his language. The alliance of wit and truth in the forum of public opinion and feeling was in significant part a creation of the *Craftsman* decades. So Johnson seems to be treating as fact a relatively recent eternal truth, the introduction of something new and oppositional in the circulation of political language and feeling. In this section, I test this hypothesis, first by exploring the real political volatility in the circumstances of *Gulliver's Travels'* publication, then by addressing the emotional dynamics of comedy and satire in some of the major passages that familiarity in the critical tradition has rendered familiar and deceptively safe. We now read the book in the light of the many children's versions in print and film that began in the nineteenth century, and the scholarly respectability of collected editions that began as early as 1735 with George Faulkner's semi-authorised Dublin edition of the *Works*. But it arrived anonymously in a world little accustomed to open and explicit political ridicule as a public function for satire.

The Fuss about *Gulliver* and Motte's Taming of the Text

Swift did not expect publication to be safe or easy. He was clearly anxious to avoid being openly identified as the author of the book that has come to be known as *Gulliver's Travels* (1726). This went beyond the routine eighteenth-century trope of anonymity, which he observed with almost all his published works. With *Gulliver*, the desire for plausible deniability of authorship was especially real and urgent, because he would be widely known to be the author and had to be able to claim innocence if formally charged. In the wake of threats of prosecution over the *Drapier's Letters*, and the death in jail of his printer John

Harding in 1725, Swift would have genuinely feared repercussions for too open an attack on present corruption. David Womersley, in the 'Textual Introduction' to *Gulliver* in the recent Cambridge Edition of Swift's *Works*, describes 'the dangers he would run by publishing his latest and most dangerous book' (Swift, 2012: 630). My account of political risk, real and apprehended, depends principally on Womersley's work, supplemented by Irvin Ehrenpreis (1962), Leo Damrosch (2013), and Paul Langford (2010). To view the book as a mobilisation of the volatile political emotions evoked by satire, we need as far as possible to unthink its current reception as a great work of literature. Now it is first met in survey courses of eighteenth-century writing or, even more anodyne, in children's books and cartoons. To get close to the public emotions mobilised in 1726, we need to imagine the personal and emotional risk of an anonymous and politically incendiary narrative.

Swift brought a manuscript of *Gulliver's Travels* 'in the hand of an amanuensis' to England from Ireland in the spring of 1726 (Swift, 2012: 632). Evidence that he had started writing it in 1721 appears in letters to Charles Ford and others, while a letter to Pope in late September 1725 announces that it was substantially complete by then (Swift, 1999: Vol. 2, 372, 606). These are the years when Walpole considered options for controlling dissent in the press and rejected censorship on pragmatic grounds rather than as a matter of principle. As Eckhart Hellmuth (2018: 160) writes:

> Walpole did not limit himself to encouraging journalism that supported his policies, but went further and also tried to obstruct the opposition press. Whether he seriously considered re-introducing the pre-censorship that had been abolished in 1695 is an open question, but it is certain that for three years, from 1722 to 1725, Walpole initiated an investigation of what additional measures could be taken to prevent criticism of his policies.

So the political ingredients of the early 1720s when Swift was writing *Gulliver* were rich. Walpole was toying with ways of suppressing dissent, while, in the other direction, Swift 'came out' as an Irish patriot in the *Drapier's Letters* and other works. All can be seen to have a common polemical purpose – *Gulliver* is the wide-scale attack on the ministry and its works to supplement the narrowcast battle for Irish liberties in the Irish pamphlets. If it was not yet fully clear to Swift that his career in the Church would go no further than the deanery of St Patrick's in Dublin, an unproductive meeting with Walpole early in his visit (on 27 April) settled that (Langford, 2010: 57). On 20 July, he wrote to James Stopford in Ireland, probably to forestall rumours about the meeting there, that 'I absolutely broke with the first Minister, and have never seen him since' (Swift, 1999: Vol. 2, 659). There would be no welcome back to political counsels in London while the Whig ascendancy lasted, and Langford avers that 'It can hardly be a coincidence that Gulliver took his first steps in public life soon afterwards' (Langford, 2010: 58).

Swift had to correspond cautiously, as letters to and from his friends of the Queen Anne days were routinely opened by the Post Office and subjected to analysis for subversive tendencies. Earl of Oxford Robert Harley had been imprisoned for two years; Henry St John, Viscount Bolingbroke, had fled to the Pretender's Court (and rather sheepishly returned in 1723 to pretend that he had only ever cared for philosophy and virtue anyway); and Bishop of Rochester Francis Atterbury had been tried in the House of Lords for treason. Opposition as a political identity was Swift's only available option for a public life, but loyal as opposed to seditious opposition was quite a new stance and function in the body politic. It provided a novel and fragile identity for the 'Patriots' around William Pulteney, who had split with Walpole in 1725, and held hopes (eventually dashed in 1727) that the Prince of Wales would usher in a different regime when he ascended to the throne. *Gulliver* was, thus, one of the early prominent acts in a wave of public dissent when it appeared in late October 1726, more than a month before the first number of the *Craftsman*, in December. It was also the first of the great Scriblerian interventions, followed in 1728 by Gay's *Beggar's Opera* and Pope's first *Dunciad* (1728). While we are today within our rights to read it as a great work of literature, it is important also to realise that it appeared in the world as a substantial rhetorical intervention in a consequential culture war.

The hugger-mugger about getting the manuscript to a printer, Benjamin Motte, and his treatment of the text seem a bizarre charade unless you take seriously the risk of post-publication sanction for sedition. Swift came to London (the first of only two trips there he took after 1714) expressly to see *Gulliver* published but, according to Womersley, 'carried with him the copy in the hand of an amanuensis presumably so he could deny authorship if the manuscript happened to be seized' (Swift, 2012: 632). He met with friends such as Pope, Gay, and Arbuthnot and may have modified the text on their advice before approaching Motte just before he returned to Dublin, through an intermediary and 'by means of a pseudonymous letter from "Richard Sympson" written in the hand of John Gay' (Swift, 2012: 633). He then agreed to terms with Motte and left London on 15 August, more than two months before the book in fact appeared. Moreover, Motte took out insurance by having many of the more apparently dangerous passages altered by Andrew Tooke, in a form Ehrenpreis (1962–83: Vol. 3, 497) goes so far as to call a 'castration' of the text. Motte protected himself against meeting

Harding's fate not by reducing the 'disgusting' passages concerning yahoos and other matters at which the Victorians took such offense. Instead, his edition did things like change the colour of the ribbons competed for in the Lilliputian court from blue, red, and green (the colours of the Garter, the Bath, and the Thistle, respectively) to the meaningless colours purple, yellow, and white (Swift, 2012: 58). Motte went to some trouble, expense, and delay to make changes to passages that pointed explicitly to court politics, so he must have hoped they provided protection from a real risk of retribution. They may or may not have been the difference that protected him, but the book was published to great acclaim and drew no direct attention from the censors.

On 7 November, Gay wrote to Swift, safely in Ireland, that ''Tis generally said that you are the Author, but I am told, the Bookseller declares he knows not from what hand it came' (Swift, 1999: Vol. 3, 47). So, it seems, the double bluff of publication and denial had worked, for both author and publisher. Swift was not happy, however, claiming on 17 November in a letter to Pope that 'his copy was basely mangled, and abused, and added to, and blotted out by the printer' (Swift, 1999: Vol. 3, 65). He saw to it that John Hyde's Dublin edition of 1726 had those restorations he could make by memory (he was without a manuscript, it seems), made some improvements to Motte's 1727 edition, then finally made further corrections for George Faulkner's edition of his collected works in 1735; by this stage, anonymity was the thinnest of residual fictions. Even so, some variant passages did not make it into print until Ravenscroft Dennis's 1899 edition, and the authenticity of the Lindalino episode (an allegorical representation of the Wood's Halfpence matter) remains disputed (Swift, 2012: 650).

Womersley makes all this superbly clear in his 'Textual Introduction' to the Cambridge *Gulliver*, and it is only in the conclusions I draw from it that I make any claim to novelty. This claim is for, literally, a recognition of the political volatility of the moment, the seriousness of the games being played to assert satirical critique without attracting prosecution for seditious libel. Swift knew that he was inviting retribution from Walpole, and the fact that it did not come does not mean that it could not have happened. Andrew Bricker (2014) has shown that fictions like blanking out the names of satirical victims were no defence at law, even though the law came gradually to be used less. The events surrounding *Gulliver*'s publication suggest that impunity depended on a nascent and fragile social licence, aided by the fact that sanctions could only be executed after publication. Suppression was harder and more obvious then, especially when the book had been so successful. In what was still broadly an honour culture, Walpole must have been very tempted to respond to the open disgust for his regime in parts of *Gulliver*. However, he seems to have understood that, as Bricker (2014: 914) puts it:

> Many simply chose not to seek redress in the courts, in large part because such redress had the capacity to raise a whole host of equally odious consequences. Going to law was a nuisance, but making oneself the undeniable butt of a joke, while also being denied the opportunity to counter a given work's accusations, was perhaps even worse. It did little to stifle the vindictive laughter such works occasioned and nothing to quash the sales public squabbles always encouraged.

This is a social and political licence to insult, not a legal one, and it obtains even today, where all politicians without a police state handy to guard their honour know that they have to roll with the satirical hits. Among recent US presidents, George W. Bush and Barack Obama mostly chose to bear with the vindictive laughter of satirical contempt, anger, and disgust by laughing along with it. Their successor responds instead with counter-anger that polarises the public but does nothing to reduce the satirical attack. This is all part of the furniture in polities where the court of public opinion and passions matters. But in Britain in the 1720s, it was a new thing, and the bravery and novelty of Swift and his publishers should not be underestimated. In this context, Johnson was making a historical statement about something relatively new when he said that Swift 'shewed that wit, confederated with truth, had such force as authority was unable to resist'. Like Swift, he wanted it to be true and so pretended that it was.

Comedy, Satire, and the Range of *Gulliver*'s Indignation

The detailed literary history in the previous section is intended to defamiliarise readers' literary assumptions about *Gulliver*, and to focus attention on it as volatile political communication. This is to some extent in parallel with Rawson's (2014: 9) work on Swift's angers where, 'There's a clear recognition that writing is a means of assuaging, not just expressing, uncontainable pressure which, he came to identify with radical human restlessness.' My goal is more social than Rawson's abstract 'radical human restlessness', but expressing and assuaging is the dual process I will come to at the end of this section in a model of satirical catharsis. The sense of political moment will permit a reading of some of the most famous bravura passages of the book, to treat them not as familiar combinations of critical cruces but, I hope, freshly as impassioned rhetoric. The rhetoric is impassioned by the CAD emotions I have been tracing throughout this book but, as Johnson has just reminded us, it is also informed by wit and humour. *Gulliver* was 'a production so new and strange, that it filled the reader with a mingled emotion of merriment and amazement'[27] (Johnson, 2014: Vol. 3, 203).

Thus far, my account of satire has avoided merriment and been pretty bleak – satire does not often tell the truth or change the world and really only reliably creates a public vent for contempt, anger, and disgust. This narrows satire to *saeva indignatio*, which can seem little more than an up-market equivalent of the cruel laughter mapped so thoroughly through the eighteenth century by Simon Dickie (2011), and abundant on the Internet today. Not even Swift is as purely indignant as this. To clarify how satire turns on the CAD triad, I have needed to separate comedy and satire for functional analytic purposes, but this is a theoretical distinction that seldom applies rigorously 'in nature'. There, as Johnson indicates, the wit necessary to raise satire from being mere abuse often looks like comic laughter, while very little actual comedy is so benign as to generate no critical laughter of judgment. The *dulce* of Horace and his imitators was nearly always mixed with some acerbic *utile*, or even just some acerbic fun.

Comedy and satire often appear in the same texts and are consequently often muddled together as cognate aspects of humour. Alternatively, they can be kept apart in a binary that contrasts pleasure-giving comedy to seriously critical dark satire. The second view is closer to the truth, in my opinion, but too schematic to be thoroughly reliable. Here is the schematic version at work, separating comedy from satire in Book I of *Gulliver's Travels*. Gulliver is a giant washed up in the land of the Lilliputians, and some of the emperor's servants are reporting on the inventory they have made of the Man Mountain's belongings:

> Out of the right Fob hung a great Silver Chain, with a wonderful kind of Engine at the Bottom. We directed him to draw out whatever was at the End of that Chain; which appeared to be a Globe, half Silver, and half of some transparent Metal: For, on the transparent Side, we saw certain strange Figures circularly drawn, and thought we could touch them, till we found our Fingers stopped by the lucid Substance. (Swift, 2012, 51–2)

So far so funny. There's a wonderful comic innocence in this defamiliarised rendition of a watch, which we see anew with a fool's clarity. The comic wonder then turns to satirical critique in the middle of the next sentence:

> He put this Engine to our Ears, which made an incessant Noise like that of a Water-Mill. And we conjecture it is either some unknown Animal, or the God that he worships: But we are more inclined to the latter Opinion, because he assured us (if we understood him right, for he expressed himself very imperfectly) that he seldom did any Thing without consulting it. He called it

---

[27] 'New and strange' is, of course, scarcely a compliment from Johnson.

his Oracle, and said it pointed out the Time for every Action of his Life.
(Swift, 2012: 52)

This is prophetic satire of clinical force, and the idea that modernity is
governed by personally regulated time has an eerie resonance that is only
becoming truer nearly three centuries later. The satirical point is clear and
twisted in the wound made by the initial incision. Satirical force can be
surgical, but it is only ever surgical as well as prolonged and excessive.
Knowingly going further and longer than is strictly necessary is so widespread
a characteristic of satire as to be functionally (if not quite absolutely) universal. A comedy of manners might stop before it goes too far, but a satire
almost never does.[28]

   It would be tempting to extrapolate from this the idea that comedy attaches to
the pleasure principle and satire to the reality principle. Satire is *utile* while
comedy is *dulce*; the critic's job is to unmix them. This would not be the
stupidest of generalisations, and it would fit very neatly with my argument
that satire is about mobilising the CAD emotions. It would be too glib, however,
because it tends to neglect the intelligence of comedy and the pleasures of satire.
A stern test for so neat a separation of satire from humour lies in the great
sentences of the King of Brobdingnag judging Gulliver and his kind, the logical
content of which presents a very bleak view of humanity. On Gulliver's second
voyage, he is stranded in a land of giants. He learns the language with his usual
bizarre facility and gets into sundry scrapes, such as failing to leap completely
over a cowpat or being used as a sex toy by maids of honour; then he enters into
discussion with the King and describes British and European culture at length.
After five audiences of exposition, the King pursues a number of queries from
his notes and sums up his horror at the account in a crescendo of judgment that
concludes thus:

> His Majesty in another Audience, was at the Pains to recapitulate the Sum of
> all I had spoken; compared the Questions he made, with the Answers I had
> given; then taking me into his Hands, and stroaking me gently, delivered
> himself in these Words, which I shall never forget, nor the Manner he spoke
> them in. My little Friend *Grildrig*; you have made a most admirable
> Panegyrick upon your Country. (Swift, 2012: 188)

Note the comic game of perspective – Grildrig/Gulliver on a giant's hand, as
ever more conscious of social niceties than physical absurdities. The King
continues to the little man on his hand:

---

[28] Consider Paul Beatty's recent prize-winning novel (Beatty, 2015). It has many brilliantly sharp
observations but they exist in a context of studied excess very characteristic of satires.

You have clearly proved that Ignorance, Idleness, and Vice are the proper Ingredients for qualifying a Legislator: That Laws are best explained, interpreted, and applied by those whose Interest and Abilities lie in perverting, confounding, and eluding them. I observe among you some Lines of an Institution, which in its Original might have been tolerable, but these half erased, and the rest wholly blurred and blotted by Corruptions. It doth not appear from all you have said, how any one Perfection is required towards the Procurement of any one Station among you; much less that Men are ennobled on Account of their Virtue, that Priests are advanced for their Piety or Learning, Soldiers for their Conduct or Valour, Judges for their Integrity, Senators for the Love of their Country, or Counsellors for their Wisdom. (Swift, 2012: 188–9)

Satire lives across time and space not so much because it fixes on eternal things, but because it can travel with eerie specificity to contexts it never imagined. Not all of the King's accusation applies to the Trump ascendancy in the United States or more thoroughly illiberal regimes such as Poland or the Philippines, but quite enough does, and it has had bite in many times since 1726. It gathers an uncanny force by being so old and still so accurate. The King concludes:

As for yourself, (continued the King) who have spent the greatest Part of your Life in travelling; I am well disposed to hope you may hitherto have escaped many Vices of your Country. But, by what I have gathered from your own Relation, and the Answers I have with much Pain wringed and extorted from you; I cannot but conclude the Bulk of your Natives to be the most pernicious Race of little odious Vermin that Nature ever suffered to crawl upon the Surface of the Earth. (Swift, 2012: 189)

This is savage indignation as sublime contempt for European humanity, and it should be utterly demoralising. It does not amount to a controlled experiment, but my classroom experience suggests otherwise. I have had students over the years who find the King's judgment simply demoralising and who write Swift off as a miserable bastard. Their response is real and perfectly valid, but the bulk of student readers experience at least some degree of exhilaration at the glorious energy of this misanthropic condemnation. In class the common response to reading it aloud is laughter, not gloom or disdain.

According to the binary between comedy and satire sketched earlier, it is possible that the rhetorical energy of the language smuggles in some comic *dulce* to leaven the astringent *utile* of the satire. It could, perhaps, be explained away as humour, though it is difficult to align tidily with any of the major categories – release, incongruity, or the sudden glory of superiority theory (Critchley, 2002). None of these categories helps explain the intense self-implication that colours the wit. What has long been described as Swift's satire of the second person is clearly evident here (Sams, 1959; Rawson, 1973;

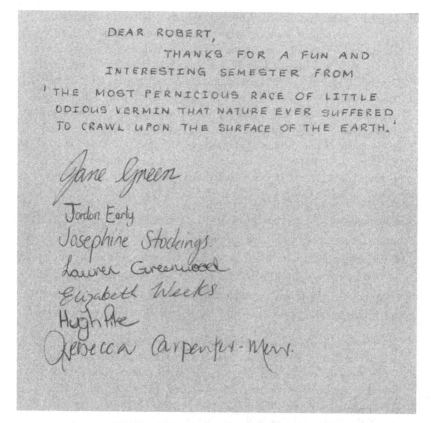

DEAR ROBERT,

THANKS FOR A FUN AND
INTERESTING SEMESTER FROM
'THE MOST PERNICIOUS RACE OF LITTLE
ODIOUS VERMIN THAT NATURE EVER SUFFERED
TO CRAWL UPON THE SURFACE OF THE EARTH.'

Jane Green
Jordon Early
Josephine Stockings
Lauren Greenwood
Elizabeth Weeks
Hugh Pike
Rebecca Carpenter-Mew

Figure 5 Personal collection of author.

Phiddian, 1995), and its bite can be seen in a gift some students gave me after one of the happiest teaching experiences of my career in 2016. With pointed affection, given how dismissive I tend to be about the children's book history of *Gulliver*, they gave me a bowdlerised copy with rather nice illustrations by Chris Riddell (2004). Figure 5 shows the inscription.

These students inhabit, cheerfully but knowingly, a logically demoralising but rhetorically vivid self-condemnation as pernicious and odious vermin. They 'get' a sort of combative wit which Thackeray and others miss when they accuse Swift of *being* disgusting rather than of mobilising disgust to satirical ends. Several followed up by writing on Swift – *Gulliver's Travels* and Atwood's *Handmaid's Tale* (1985) (another dark satire) was the most popular combination – in the long essay the course was designed to foster.

Amid the King's cosmic gloom of disgust, anger, and contempt, there is the conflicted pleasure of satire, a sort of sour and intelligent exuberance that uses wit for charismatic destruction of illusions. Obviously, this is not true of all satire, much of which is 'easy' enough to explain through superiority theory where one sits with Juvenal or Pope among the elect enraged by the depravity of the world. Satire can, in other words, be a display of moralising righteousness that invites complicit judgmental laughter. But there is a sort of satire that comes to get you and implicates you in the madness that abounds; a recent example might be Hannah Gadsby's *Nanette* (2018), which blows up heteronormative male stand-up comedy with excruciating hilarity. For me and my favourite vermin, it seems, there is a joy that belongs with the emotional pain.

The sternest test for this rather buoyant view of emotional resilience in the face of satirical apocalypse is presented by Gulliver among the Yahoos. As Johnson (2014: 203) avers, rather dismissively, 'that which gave most disgust must be the history of the *Houyhnhnms*.' No account of *Gulliver* in the light of the CAD triad can ignore passages from the fourth book like this description of Yahoo politics by the Houyhnhnm Master:

> He had heard indeed some curious *Houyhnhnms* observe, that in most Herds there was a Sort of ruling *Yahoo*, (as among us there is generally some leading or principal Stag in a Park) who was always more *deformed* in Body, and *mischievous in Disposition*, than any of the rest. That, this *Leader* had usually a Favourite as *like himself* as he could get, whose Employment was to *lick his Master's Feet and Posteriors, and drive the Female* Yahoos *to his Kennel*; for which he is now and then rewarded with a Piece of Ass's Flesh. (Swift, 2012: 394)

Attention to Swift's supposed 'excremental vision' (Brown, 1959; and much subsequent psychoanalytically tinged Swift criticism) should not distract readers from the fairly obvious identification of the King and his First Minister here. To call the King deformed, lascivious, and mischievous is impertinent enough; then hostile attention turns to his arse-licking off-sider, on whom wish-fulfilling punishment is visited:

> This *Favourite* is hated by the whole Herd; and therefore to protect himself, keeps always *near the Person of his Leader*. He usually continues in Office till a worse can be found; but the very Moment he is discarded, his Successor, at the Head of all the *Yahoos* of the District, Young and Old, Male and Female, come in a Body, and discharge their Excrements upon him from head to Foot. (Swift 2012: 394–5)

This is an exemplar of psychological disgust, combining all four aspects posited by Rozin, Haidt, and McCauley (2008; see Section 2): core disgust in the oral incorporation from the arse-licking, animal-nature disgust in the shitting, interpersonal disgust in the ostracism, and moral disgust in the ritual nature of it all. The political specifics of this revelling in excrement are conditioned a little for

Swift by bitterness at the aftermath of the fall of Queen Anne's last ministry, but this is primarily a defiant mobilisation of disgust at a figure very like Walpole, and a prophesy of his humiliating demise. It marks also a durable tendency in parliamentary systems to discard leaders more harshly than is reasonably necessary. This sort of anger and disgust often tinges the emotions evinced in the public by those who gain and lose political power.

Certainly, the idea of a public shitting on ex-leaders runs the risk of causing cynical disengagement in the public, which is a public emotion, but a politically limited one. Satire has no silver bullet protection to make it behave reliably as Pope's 'Sacred Weapon'. It can heap ordure on opponents, or scurrilously cast aspersions on their sexual habits. But it can also rise to visionary anger and disgust, when Swift uses his Irish experience to explode the delusions of European imperialism in midstream. At the end of the fourth voyage, Gulliver explains why he has neglected to claim the many lands he has visited for the British Crown:

> To say the Truth, I had conceived a few Scruples with relation to the distributive Justice of Princes upon those Occasions. For Instance, A Crew of Pyrates are driven by a Storm they know not whither; at length a Boy discovers Land from the Top-mast; they go on Shore to rob and plunder, they see an harmless People, are entertained with Kindness; they give the Country a new Name, they take formal Possession of it for the King, they set up a rotten Plank, or a Stone, for a Memorial, they murder two or three Dozen of the Natives, bring away a Couple more by Force for a Sample, return home, and get their Pardon. Here commences a new Dominion acquired with a Title by *Divine Right*. Ships are sent with the first Opportunity; the Natives driven out or destroyed, their Princes tortured to discover their Gold; a free Licence given to all Acts of Inhumanity and Lust; the Earth reeking with the Blood of its Inhabitants: And this execrable Crew of Butchers employed in so pious an Expedition, is a *modern Colony*, sent to convert and civilize an idolatrous and barbarous People. (Swift, 2012: 440–1)

This template of colonial deprivation mobilises anger at the 'execrable Crew of Butchers' and all who profit from their piracy. It also seeks to shame readers into recognising the injustice of colonialism and the common humanity of the 'Natives' brought to civilisation. Among the twenty-first century ethicists of emotion, Macalester Bell (2013) would certainly justify this as 'apt contempt' for those who commit the imperial crimes and also for those who paper over them with the deceptive rhetoric civilisation and conversion. Martha Nussbaum (2016) might even give it a pass as 'transition anger', the only part of the CAD triad she will tolerate in her Houyhnhnm-like equanimity. But it is also a calculated affront to King George so plain that Gulliver immediately draws attention to the personal (and especially the Irish) dimension by ineptly explaining the insult away in the next (less famous) paragraph:

> But this Description, I confess, does by no means affect the *British* Nation, who may be an Example to the whole World for their Wisdom, Care, and Justice in planting Colonies; their liberal Endowments for the Advancement of Religion and Learning; their Choice of devout and able Pastors to propagate *Christianity*; their Caution in stocking their Provinces with People of sober Lives and Conversations from this the Mother Kingdom; their strict Regard to the Distribution of Justice, in supplying the Civil Administration through all their Colonies with Officers of the greatest Abilities, utter Strangers to Corruption: And, to crown all, by sending the most vigilant and virtuous Governors, who have no other Views than the Happiness of the People over whom they preside, and the Honour of the King their Master. (Swift, 2012: 441–2)

Everything becomes a sort of list at the end of Book IV, with one thing tumbling after another in a mounting pile of rage that is Gulliver's madness and Swift's anger. Here the satirical relentlessness twists the knife in the incision made by the previous paragraph again and again. The initial irony, implausibly denying that this refers to British rule, is plain sarcasm. The list is a litany of what Swift thought wrong in British rule in Ireland, and a premonition of Edmund Burke's strictures on rule in India (Herron, 2012; Whelan, 2012). Swift is venting his indignation and taking a real risk that the formal irony's thin veil of plausible deniability will not be challenged by affronted authorities. That he and others got away with it was integral to the establishment of new norms for public critique and emotion, norms that had little legal protection but enjoyed a social licence that has endured.

Satirical Catharsis

I have done the critical and descriptive 'show' in this section before proceeding to the 'tell' of theoretical analysis. According to most rules of academic discourse, this is to put the cart before the horse, but my aim has been to ground readers thoroughly in the experience of what I want to explain before seeking the perspective of analytic mastery. By now, you should be persuaded that contempt, anger, and disgust (broadly understood) mark the cognitive territory (i.e. a range of thought and emotion) of a dominant element in satirical texts. This theoretical orientation situates satire in effect rather than form and allows for a lot of functional separation of comedy and satire, even where they cohabit in the same texts. So how, again broadly, does satire work to express or contain the public and political emotions?

In the passages discussed here, Swift mobilises contempt, anger, and disgust at the moral smallness and myopia of European civilisation, but to what ends? The King of Brobdingnag's great judgment expresses contempt, thus eliciting anger in Gulliver, who finds 'my noble and most beloved Country … so injuriously treated' (Swift, 2012: 190), and in those who reject Swift as a misanthropist, from Thackeray to my gentler students. Meanwhile, Swift's engaged reader is, in my account, drawn into a rich and somehow liberating play of self-disgust, something that invites us to recognise and recoil from corruption in the world around us, and *possibly* to seek reform. This is schematic and a nuanced cultural criticism will necessarily reach for a wider palette of words such as disdain, horror, and bemusement to give more precise accounts. It is, nevertheless, clear that in the zone defined by the CAD triad we have the broad emotional territory of satire and, particularly, a robust model for what separates it from the gentler and more celebratory forms of humour that one associates with comedy. This separation obtains whether or not the satire is 'correctly' understood according to the plausibly retrievable intention of its creator. In the real world of political and cultural debate, 'getting' satire is less a matter of skilled interpretation than of using a text to exercise moralising or judgmental emotions in a notionally playful context. One can be revolted, uneasily implicated, or delighted by the King's great sentence, but it acts as a satirical provocation even if different publics construct its meaning incompatibly.

This complex internal theatre of the emotions can seldom be mobilised reliably, as the wildly mixed reactions to satirical provocations as complex as Rushdie's *Satanic Verses* and as primitive as the *Jyllands-Posten*'s cartoons of Mohammed suggest. Yet very often satire has limited controversial or political impact, even while mobilising these strong negative emotions. Satires which meet and affirm their public's views but bring no visible change are still doing cultural work in the wider ecology of freeish presses. Here an analogy with tragedy helps to understand something that I used to find disturbing and which now I view with mixed feelings, the consolatory delights of satire.

According to Aristotle in the *Poetics*, 'tragedy is an imitation not just of a complete action, but of events that evoke pity and fear' (Aristotle 2013: 29). The purpose of this imitation ('mimesis') is to make an audience enjoy the purgation or purification or clarification ('katharsis' remains a disputed word for which Aristotle never provides an explicit definition) of those terrible emotions. This tells only part of the story of the pleasure we take in tragedy, which is why the argument has been endlessly debated over the centuries, but it does tell a fundamental part. It points to the moral and aesthetic pleasure that lies unsettlingly at the root of tragedy. My proposition here is that something similar to this often happens in the mobilisation of the satirical CAD triad – a catharsis of negative emotions that can purge, purify, or clarify contempt, anger, and disgust for agents in the satirical engagement, both authors and their various audiences. The King of Brobdingnag's great peroration, which I have read hundreds of times, silently and aloud, alone and in the company of students, gives me a sort of angry joy that is yet to drive me out on a mission to obliterate the vermin, and it never leaves me gloomy. The excremental political habits of the Yahoos I find amusing, perhaps because they literalise metaphors for conduct that remains visible in politics and, dare I say, universities to this day. The attacks on colonialism I find exhilarating, if also challenging as a prosperous European member of what used until recently to be called a settler society. None of these emotional reactions seems to me morally or politically debilitating, to sponsor *mere* cynicism. I have gone to some lengths throughout this Element to separate the satirical from the humorous but must concede now that this separation cannot be maintained absolutely. Even the darkest satire turns on wit (and very often humour) as well as on the mobilisation of harsh emotions. Without the wit, it becomes mere abuse or complaint.

So, this study's final proposition is that satirical catharsis is often a theatre of emotion that performs a useful civic function as a performative consolation for the morally distressed, the *indignados*. My account of the Scriblerians thus presents early-eighteenth-century polemics as a crucible for the historical development of this social more than legal licence. The effect of a satire can be energising and even liberating, but it only rarely generates direct political action, either in the form of an uprising against the dominant knaves and fools or satisfyingly devastating self-reflection on their part. Walpole did not like what Swift wrote, but it seems to have had no more than marginal influence on his manner of governing, or his success. He is a strange sort of hero in my cultural narrative because he chose to brazen out the satirical critique and not to suppress it. Clearly he decided that his honour could look after itself as his command of the institutions meant he could contest or ignore the abuse. Indeed, he might have looked stronger politically for appearing to enjoy the joke. This is a normal assumption of electoral politics now, but it was novel then. *Gulliver* did not succeed in defeating Walpole or the many ills Swift diagnosed through its pages. Satires seldom achieve their apparent worldly purposes, even when they provide abiding moral and aesthetic release for the passions. We can enjoy the cathartic pleasures of Swift's greatest satire still as a literary experience but should also appreciate its volatility in its moment, the personal risk it entailed, and its political achievement as a harbinger of toleration for satires to come.

Epilogue: Satire in the Digital Age

This Element started with a speculative myth of the origins of political satire as an embodied thing in the confrontation between Aristophanes and Cleon before the citizens of Athens. Its body focuses on satire and the harsh public emotions in the print age, particularly the formative moment for satirical liberty in early-eighteenth-century Britain. Now, however, satire faces the general twenty-first-century problem of being a practice developed in a world of scarcity (especially of communication platforms) entering a world of content profusion. The national public spheres defined by mass media are fracturing into myriad digital publics through social media. These new publics are both potentially universal in their reach and micro-selective for ideological partisanship. For example, in the old world of newspapers with distinct markets, a cartoon about a tennis match published in the Melbourne *Herald-Sun* would have been hard pressed to reach an audience even across Australia. Now, as Mark Knight discovered in 2018, his cartoon of Serena Williams at the US Open could be taken up into a huge (if brief) vortex of international controversy and outrage for perceived racism.[29] As I was writing this epilogue, news broke that the *New York Times* had decided to stop publishing cartoons in its international edition, for fear of causing offense in unexpected places. All this has consequences for political satire, and I close with some preliminary speculations on how two of the most prominent politicians of the current decade, Barack Obama and Donald Trump, have sought to manage them. These thoughts are emblematic but may suggest some continuities and differences in the effects of satire at this moment of media transition and provoke further scholarly debate.

On 8 December 2014, Barack Obama appeared as himself on the *Colbert Report* and 'took over' to launch a 'decree' about his controversial healthcare plan. Despite some tricky residual ironies from the parodic news program's mode, he successfully co-opted the platform to defuse his reputation for aloofness and show a 'self-aware sense of humour' (Higgie, 2017: 90). The account on the White House website shows a transparent political desire to reach a voter demographic and have 'the final word – or decree – on health care':

> Most young people can get covered for less than $100. How is the President going to get that message out to the kids? He could try to appeal to them directly through a speech or a press conference, but young people don't watch real news shows like this one. They watch comedy shows, and I just don't see the President going on one of those. They're beneath his dignity. (Somanader, 2014)

---

[29] See Scully, 2018.

This is the Walpole method – cosying up to tractable parts of the media and looking like a good sport. It seeks to diffuse public emotion through comedy and self-irony to turn it to political ends. Political rationality remains the governing frame for humour that seeks to subordinate emotional force. The rumour at the time was that young people get their news from comedy and satire rather than traditional media outlets, so this is a canny attempt to reach a public that may be crucial for policy and electoral reasons.[30] Obama reframed his natural reserve, as a sort of ironic coolness. He did so for utterly traditional political reasons.

Donald Trump, by contrast, revels in the combative public emotions. He mobilises the CAD triad among both his supporters and his opponents and has engaged in a long Twitter war with the satirical television program *Saturday Night Live* (Becker, 2018). In Alec Baldwin's regular impersonation, he is presented as an orange-haired buffoon, vain and intemperate. In turn, he vainly and intemperately accuses the show of being 'sad' and 'not funny'. He meets anger with anger, contempt with contempt. And because he does not play by any of the recognised shaming conventions of US political life, it works for him politically. In an already polarised political environment, he enrages his opponents and encourages his allies. British protestors reprised this situation when the president visited the UK in 2019 and they flew the blow-up Trump baby in the London skies (Figure 6). It

Figure 6 A giant baby Trump balloon flies over Parliament Square during a demonstration against Donald Trump's visit to the UK on 13 July 2018. Photograph by TF-Images / Getty Images.

---

[30] See Gray, Jones, and Thompson, 2009.

worked as satirical catharsis, but in a paradoxically divided way. It is apprehended viscerally as true by opponents of Trump and viscerally as false by his supporters. Both groups are strengthened in their political allegiances, and very few people are likely to be converted. Meanwhile Trump himself has built a political persona that thrives on conflict rather than reconciliation, so he profits from the insult.

Trump's may be a rare triumph for political shamelessness, but it demonstrates my main point: satire mobilises the CAD emotions in public, but the results can be hard to control. Satire is an almost universal element of political life, but it is more often a vehicle for emotional catharsis than a silver bullet for change or truth. In the print age, it provided a play space for intemperate critique and a public forum for emotional spectacle; in doing so, it supported a freeish press in many countries. Today many (including myself) fear that the 'general public' will be sucked into ideological mono-cultures by the market-segmenting logic of social media. Should that happen, satires will only aid an epidemic of emotional confirmation bias that narrow emotional publics incite. If some public space for debate and dispute is kept alive, however, there will continue to be plenty of stabilising emotional work for satire to do.

References

Appignanesi, Lisa, and Sara Maitland. (1990). *The Rushdie File*. Syracuse, NY: Syracuse University Press.

Aristophanes. (2011). *Acharnians, Knights, and, Peace*. Translated by Michael Ewans. Norman: University of Oklahoma Press.

Aristotle. (1705). *Aristotle's Art of Poetry. Translated from the Original Greek, According to Mr. Theodore Goulston's Edition. Together, with Mr. D'Acier's Notes Translated from the French*. Edited by André Dacier, London: British Library.

(2013). *Poetics*. Oxford: Oxford University Press.

Averill, J. R. (2012). Anger. In V. S. Ramachandran, ed., *Encyclopedia of Human Behavior*, 2nd edn. San Diego: Academic Press, pp. 137–44. https://doi.org/10.1016/B978-0–12-375000–6.00023–9.

Bacon, Francis. (1954). *Figure with Meat*. Art Institute Chicago. www.artic.edu/artworks/4884/figure-with-meat.

Barrett, Lisa Feldman. (2006). Are Emotions Natural Kinds? *Perspectives on Psychological Science*, **1**(1), 28–58. https://doi.org/10.1111/j.1745–6916.2006.00003.x.

Baumgartner, Jody C., and Jonathan S. Morris. (2008). One 'Nation,' Under Stephen? The Effects of *The Colbert Report* on American Youth. *Journal of Broadcasting & Electronic Media*, **52**(4), 622–43. https://doi.org/10.1080/08838150802437487.

Baumgartner, Jody C., Jonathan S. Morris, and Natasha L. Walth. (2012). The Fey Effect: Young Adults, Political Humor, and Perceptions of Sarah Palin in the 2008 Presidential Election Campaign. *Public Opinion Quarterly*, **76**(1), 95–104. https://doi.org/10.1093/poq/nfr060.

Beatty, Paul. (2015). *The Sellout: A Novel*. New York: Farrar, Straus and Giroux.

Becker, Amy B. (2018). Live From New York, It's Trump on Twitter! The Effect of Engaging With Saturday Night Live on Perceptions of Authenticity and the Salience of Trait Ratings. *International Journal of Communication*, **12**, 1736–57.

Bell, Macalester. (2013). *Hard Feelings: The Moral Psychology of Contempt*. Oxford: Oxford University Press.

Black, Jeremy, ed. (1984). *Britain in the Age of Walpole*. Basingstoke, Hampshire: Macmillan.

Boswell, James. (2014). *Boswell's Life of Johnson*. Vol. 2, *The Life (1766–1776)*. Edited by George Birkbeck, Norman Hill, and Lawrence Fitzroy Powell. Oxford: Oxford University Press.

Boyd, Brian. (2009). *On the Origin of Stories: Evolution, Cognition, and Fiction*. Cambridge, MA: Belknap Press of Harvard University Press.

Bricker, Andrew Benjamin. (2014). Libel and Satire: The Problem with Naming. *ELH*, **81**(3), 889–921. https://doi.org/10.1353/elh.2014.0026.

Brown, Norman O. (1959). *Life against Death: The Psychoanalytical Meaning of History*. London: Routledge.

Carroll, Joseph. (2004). *Literary Darwinism: Evolution, Human Nature, and Literature*. New York: Routledge.

Chapman, Hanah A., and Adam K. Anderson. (2012). Understanding Disgust. *Annals of the New York Academy of Sciences*, **1251**(1), 62–76. https://doi.org/10.1111/j.1749–6632.2011.06369.x.

(2013). Things Rank and Gross in Nature: A Review and Synthesis of Moral Disgust. *Psychological Bulletin*, **139**(2), 300–327. https://doi.org/10.1037/a0030964.

Chen, Khin Wee, Robert Phiddian, and Ronald Stewart. (2017). Towards a Discipline of Political Cartoon Studies: Mapping the Field. In Jessica Milner Davis, ed., *Satire and Politics: The Interplay of Heritage and Practice*. London: Palgrave Macmillan, pp. 125–62. https://doi.org/10.1007/978-3-319-56774-7_5.

Clark, Jason, and Daniel Fessler. (2015). The Role of Disgust in Norms, and of Norms in Disgust Research: Why Liberals Shouldn't Be Morally Disgusted by Moral Disgust. *Topoi: An International Review of Philosophy*, **34**(2), 483–98. https://doi.org/10.1007/s11245-014-9240-0.

Condren, Conal. (2009). Public, Private and the Idea of the 'Public Sphere' in Early–Modern England. *Intellectual History Review*, **19**(1), 15–28. https://doi.org/10.1080/17496970902722866.

(2012). Satire and Definition. *Humor: International Journal of Humor Research*, **25**(4), 375–99.

Critchley, Simon. (2002). *On Humour*. London: Routledge.

Damrosch, Leopold. (2013). *Jonathan Swift: His Life and His World*. New Haven: Yale University Press.

D'Anvers, Caleb, ed. (1731). *The Craftsman*. 14 vols. London: Printed for R. Francklin. http://galenet.galegroup.com/servlet/MOME?af=RN&ae=U100676401&srchtp=a&ste=14&q=nla.

Dastani, Mehdi, and Alexander Pankov. (2017). Other-Condemning Moral Emotions: Anger, Contempt and Disgust. *ACM Transactions on Internet Technology*, **17**(1), 4:1–4:24. https://doi.org/10.1145/2998570.

Dickie, Simon. (2011). *Cruelty and Laughter: Forgotten Comic Literature and the Unsentimental Eighteenth Century*. Chicago: University of Chicago Press.

Dubreuil, Benoît. (2010). Punitive Emotions and Norm Violations. *Philosophical Explorations*, **13**(1), 35–50. https://doi.org/10.1080/13869790903486776.

(2015). Anger and Morality. *Topoi: An International Review of Philosophy*, **34**(2), 475–82. https://doi.org/10.1007/s11245-014–9238-7.

Dutton, Denis. (2009). *The Art Instinct: Beauty, Pleasure, & Human Evolution*. New York: Bloomsbury Press.

Ehrenpreis, Irvin. (1962–83). *Swift: The Man, His Works, and the Age*. 3 vols. London: Methuen.

Elias, Norbert. (1978). *The Civilizing Process*. Oxford: Blackwell.

Elliott, Robert C. (1960). *The Power of Satire: Magic, Ritual, Art*. Princeton: Princeton University Press.

Erskine-Hill, Howard. (1981). Alexander Pope: The Political Poet in His Time. *Eighteenth-Century Studies*, **15**(2), 123–48. https://doi.org/10.2307/2738239.

Eschenbaum, Natalie K., and Barbara Correll, eds. (2016). *Disgust in Early Modern English Literature*. London: Routledge.

Flanagan, Owen. (2018). Introduction: The Moral Psychology of Anger. In Myisha Cherry and Owen Flanagan, eds., *The Moral Psychology of Anger*. London: Rowman and Littlefield, pp. vii–xxxi.

Gay, John. (2013). *The Beggar's Opera and Polly*. Edited by Hal Gladfelder. Oxford: Oxford University Press.

Gerrard, Christine. (1994). *The Patriot Opposition to Walpole: Politics, Poetry, and National Myth, 1725–1742*. Oxford: Clarendon Press.

Gervais, Matthew M., and Daniel M. T. Fessler. (2017). On the Deep Structure of Social Affect: Attitudes, Emotions, Sentiments, and the Case of 'Contempt'. *Behavioral and Brain Sciences*, **40**, 1–63. https://doi.org/10.1017/S0140525X16000352.

Gillray, James. (1796). National Conveniences. Etching. British Museum. www.britishmuseum.org/research/collection_online/collection_object_details.aspx?objectId=1601167&partId=1&searchText=gillray+national+convenience&page=1.

Gray, Jonathan, Jeffrey P. Jones, and Ethan Thompson. (2009). *Satire TV: Politics and Comedy in the Post-Network Era*. New York: New York University Press.

Greenberg, Jonathan. (2018). *The Cambridge Introduction to Satire*. Cambridge: Cambridge University Press.

Gutierrez, Roberto, and Roger Giner-Sorolla. (2007). Anger, Disgust, and Presumption of Harm as Reactions to Taboo-Breaking Behaviors. *Emotion*, **7**(4): 853–68. https://doi.org/10.1037/1528–3542.7.4.853.

Habermas, Jurgen. (1989). *The Structural Transformation of the Public Sphere: An Inquiry into a Category of Bourgeois Society*. Cambridge, MA: MIT Press.

Haidt, Jonathan. (2003). The Moral Emotions. In R. J. Davidson, K. R. Scherer, H. H. Goldsmith, eds., *Handbook of Affective Sciences*. Oxford: Oxford University Press, pp. 852–70.

(2012). *The Righteous Mind: Why Good People Are Divided by Politics and Religion*. London: Allen Lane.

Hammond, Brean S. (1984). *Pope and Bolingbroke: A Study of Friendship and Influence*. Columbia: University of Missouri Press.

Hellmuth, Eckhart. (2018). Towards Hume – the Discourse on the Liberty of the Press in the Age of Walpole. *History of European Ideas*, **44**(2), 159–81. https://doi.org/10.1080/01916599.2018.1429730.

Henrich, Joseph, Steven J. Heine, and Ara Norenzayan. (2010). The Weirdest People in the World? *Behavioral and Brain Sciences*, **33**(2–3), 61–83. https://doi.org/10.1017/S0140525X0999152X.

Herron, Shane. (2012). Burke and Swift on the Ethics of Revolution. *SEL Studies in English Literature 1500–1900*, **52**(3), 669–96. https://doi.org/10.1353/sel.2012.0028.

Hervey, John, Lord. (1855). *Memoirs of the Reign of George the Second, from His Accession to the Death of Queen Caroline*. London: J. Murray.

Herz, Rachel. (2012). *That's Disgusting: Unraveling the Mysteries of Repulsion*. New York: W. W. Norton & Co.

Higgie, Rebecca. (2017). Under the Guise of Humour and Critique: The Political Co-Option of Popular Contemporary Satire. In Jessica Milner Davis, ed., *Satire and Politics: The Interplay of Heritage and Practice*. London: Palgrave Macmillan, pp. 73–102. https://doi.org/10.1007/978-3-319-56774-7_3.

Hobbes, Thomas. (1991). *Leviathan. Cambridge Texts in the History of Political Thought*. Cambridge; New York: Cambridge University Press.

Hultquist, Aleksondra. (2017). The Passions. In Susan Broomhall, ed., *Early Modern Emotions: An Introduction*. London: Routledge, pp. 71–73.

Hume, David. (2008). *An Enquiry Concerning Human Understanding*. Edited by P. J. R Millican. Oxford: Oxford University Press.

(2011). *A Treatise of Human Nature: A Critical Edition*. Edited by David Fate Norton and Mary J. Norton. Oxford: Clarendon.

Hutcherson, Cendri A., and James J. Gross. 2011. The Moral Emotions: A Social–Functionalist Account of Anger, Disgust, and Contempt. *Journal of Personality and Social Psychology*, **100**(4), 719–37. https://doi.org/10.1037/a0022408.

Iuvenalis, Decimus Iunius. (1996). *Juvenal: Satires.* Edited by Susan M. Braund. Cambridge: Cambridge University Press.

Jenkins, Martin. (2004). *Jonathan Swift's Gulliver.* London: Walker Books. https://trove.nla.gov.au/work/9919867.

Johnson, Samuel. (2014). *The Lives of the Most Eminent English Poets with Critical Observations on Their Works.* Edited by Roger H. Lonsdale. 4 vols. Oxford: Oxford University Press.

Kahneman, Daniel. (2011). *Thinking, Fast and Slow.* London: Allen Lane.

Kelly, Daniel R. (2011). *Yuck!: The Nature and Moral Significance of Disgust.* Cambridge, MA: MIT Press.

Kemp, Geoff. (2012). The 'End of Censorship' and the Politics of Toleration, from Locke to Sacheverell. *Parliamentary History*, **31**(1), 47–68. https://doi.org/10.1111/j.1750–0206.2011.00282.x.

Kerr, David S. (2000). *Caricature and French Political Culture 1830–1848 : Charles Philipon and the Illustrated Press.* Oxford: Clarendon Press.

Kinservik, Matthew J. (2002). *Disciplining Satire: The Censorship of Satiric Comedy on the Eighteenth-Century London Stage.* Lewisburg, PA: Bucknell University Press.

Klausen, Jytte. (2009). *The Cartoons That Shook the World.* New Haven: Yale University Press.

Knight, Charles A. (2004). *The Literature of Satire.* Cambridge: Cambridge University Press.

Knights, Mark. (2007). How Rational Was the Later Stuart Public Sphere? In Peter Lake and Steven Pincus, eds., *The Politics of the Public Sphere in Early Modern England.* Manchester: Manchester University Press, pp. 252–67.

Kollareth, Dolichan, and James Russell. (2017). On the Emotions Associated with Violations of Three Moral Codes (Community, Autonomy, Divinity). *Motivation and Emotion* **41**(3), 322–42. https://doi.org/10.1007/s11031-017–9611-0.

(2019). Disgust and the Sacred: Do People React to Violations of the Sacred With the Same Emotion They React to Something Putrid? *Emotion*, **19**(1), 37–52. https://doi.org/10.1037/emo0000412.

Korsmeyer, Carolyn. (2011). *Savoring Disgust: The Foul and the Fair in Aesthetics.* New York: Oxford University Press.

Lake, Peter, and Steve Pincus. (2006). Rethinking the Public Sphere in Early Modern England. *Journal of British Studies*, **45**(2), 270–92. https://doi.org/10.1086/499788.

Lake, Peter, and Steven Pincus, eds. (2007). *The Politics of the Public Sphere in Early Modern England.* Manchester: Manchester University Press.

Lamarre, Heather, Kristen Landreville, and Michael Beam. (2009). The Irony of Satire: Political Ideology and the Motivation to See What You Want to See in *The Colbert Report*. *The International Journal of Press/Politics*, **14**(2), 212–31. https://doi.org/10.1177/1940161208330904.

Langford, Paul. (2010). Swift and Walpole. In Claude Rawson, ed., *Politics and Literature in the Age of Swift: English and Irish Perspectives*. Cambridge: Cambridge University Press, pp. 52–78.

Lateiner, Donald, and Dimos Spatharas. (2016). *The Ancient Emotion of Disgust*. Oxford: Oxford University Press.

Love, Harold. (2004). *English Clandestine Satire 1660–1702*. Oxford: Oxford University Press.

Lund, Roger. (2016). 'An Alembick of Innuendos': Satire, Libel, and The Craftsman. *Philological Quarterly*, **95**(2), 243–68.

Mack, Maynard. (1985). *Alexander Pope: A Life*. New Haven: Yale University Press.

Manning, Haydon, and Robert Phiddian. (2013). Following and Recalling Election Campaigns through Cartoons. *The Conversation*. http://theconver sation.com/following-and-recalling-election-campaigns-through-car toons-16575.

Marshall, Ashley. (2013). *The Practice of Satire in England, 1658–1770*. Baltimore: Johns Hopkins University Press.

Mason, Michelle. (2010). On Shamelessness. *Philosophical Papers*, **39**(3), 401–25. https://doi.org/10.1080/05568641.2010.538916.

    ed. (2018). *The Moral Psychology of Contempt*. Lanham, MD: Rowman and Littlefield. https://ws1.nbni.co.uk/widgets/page/5ac62a31f5ba7400784e8730/0.

McBain, Jean. (2019). Liberty, Licentiousness and Libel: The London Newspaper 1695–1742. PhD, Melbourne, Victoria: University of Melbourne.

McLuhan, Eric. (2015). *Cynic Satire*. Newcastle-upon-Tyne: Cambridge Scholars Publishing.

Menninghaus, Winfried. (2003). *Disgust: The Theory and History of a Strong Sensation*. Albany: State University of New York Press.

Miceli, Maria, and Cristiano Castelfranchi. (2018). Contempt and Disgust: The Emotions of Disrespect. *Journal for the Theory of Social Behaviour*, **48**(2), 205–29. https://doi.org/10.1111/jtsb.12159.

    (2019). Anger and Its Cousins. *Emotion Review*, **11**(1), 13–26. https://doi.org/10.1177/1754073917714870.

Miller, William Ian. (1997). *The Anatomy of Disgust*. Cambridge, MA: Harvard University Press.

Musgrave, David. (2014). *Grotesque Anatomies: Menippean Satire since the Renaissance*. Newcastle upon Tyne: Cambridge Scholars Publishing.

Ngai, Sianne. (2014). *Ugly Feelings*. Cambridge, MA: Harvard University Press.

Nokes, David. (1995). *John Gay, a Profession of Friendship*. Oxford: Oxford University Press.

Novak, Maximillian E. (2001). *Daniel Defoe: Master of Fictions: His Life and Ideas*. Oxford: Oxford University Press.

Nussbaum, Martha Craven. (2004). *Hiding from Humanity: Disgust, Shame, and the Law*. Princeton: Princeton University Press.

(2016). *Anger and Forgiveness: Resentment, Generosity, Justice*. Oxford: Oxford University Press.

(2018). *The Monarchy of Fear: A Philosopher Looks at Our Political Crisis*. Oxford: Oxford University Press.

Pagden, Anthony. (2013). *The Enlightenment: And Why It Still Matters*. New York: Random House.

Parrott, W. Gerrod. (2012). Ur-Emotions: The Common Feature of Animal Emotions and Socially Constructed Emotions. *Emotion Review*, **4**(3), 247–8. https://doi.org/10.1177/1754073912439786.

2016. Psychological Perspectives on Emotion in Groups. In Heather Kerr, David Lemmings, and Robert Phiddian, eds., *Passions, Sympathy and Print Culture: Public Opinion and Emotional Authenticity in Eighteenth-Century Britain*. London: Palgrave Macmillan, pp. 20–44. https://doi.org/10.1057/9781137455413_2.

Pearce, Edward. (2007). *The Great Man: Scoundrel, Genius and Britain's First Prime Minister*. London: Jonathan Cape.

Pfaff, Kerry L., and Raymond W. Gibbs. (1997). Authorial Intentions in Understanding Satirical Texts. *Poetics*, **25**(1), 45–70. https://doi.org/10.1016/S0304-422X(97)00006-5.

Phiddian, Robert. (1995). *Swift's Parody*. Cambridge: Cambridge University Press.

(2011). 'Strange Lengths': Hume and Satire in the Dialogues Concerning Natural Religion. In Craig Taylor and Stephen Buckle, eds., *Hume and the Enlightenment*. London: Pickering & Chatto, pp. 91–104.

(2013). Satire and the Limits of Literary Theories. *Critical Quarterly*, **55**(3), 44–58. https://doi.org/10.1111/criq.12057.

(2016). The Emotional Contents of Swift's *Saeva Indignatio*. In Heather Kerr, David Lemmings, and Robert Phiddian, eds., *Passions, Sympathy and Print Culture: Public Opinion and Emotional Authenticity in Eighteenth-Century Britain*. London: Palgrave Macmillan UK, pp. 47–67. https://doi.org/10.1057/9781137455413_3.

(2017). Spectacular Opposition: Suppression, Deflection and the Performance of Contempt in John Gay's *Beggar's Opera* and *Polly*. In Mark Knights and Adam Morton, eds., *The Power of Laughter and Satire in Early Modern Britain: Political and Religious Culture, 1500–1820*. Woodbridge, Suffolk: Boydell & Brewer, pp. 133–51. https://doi.org/ 10.1017/9781787440814.007.

Phiddian, Robert, and Haydon R. Manning. (2008). *Comic Commentators: Contemporary Political Cartooning in Australia*. Perth, WA: Network.

Phiddian, Robert, and Jean McBain. (2017). Emotional and Scribal Communities in the Verses on the Death of Dr. Swift. *The Eighteenth Century: Theory and Interpretation*, **58**(3), 353.

Pinker, Steven. (2011). *The Better Angels of Our Nature: Why Violence Has Declined*. New York: Viking.

Plamper, Jan. (2015). *The History of Emotions: An Introduction*. Translated by Keith Tribe. Oxford: Oxford University Press.

Plumb, J. H. (1956). *Sir Robert Walpole: The Making of a Statesman*. London: Cresset Press.

(1960). *Sir Robert Walpole: The King's Minister*. London: Cresset Press.

Pollard, Mary. (2000). *A Dictionary of Members of the Dublin Book Trade 1550–1800*. London: Bibliographical Society.

Pope, Alexander. (1963). *The Poems of Alexander Pope: A One-Volume Edition of the Twickenham Text with Selected Annotations*. London: Methuen.

Rabb, Melinda Alliker. (2007). *Satire and Secrecy in English Literature from 1650 to 1750*. New York: Palgrave Macmillan.

Rawson, Claude Julien. (1973). *Gulliver and the Gentle Reader; Studies in Swift and Our Time*. London: Routledge & Kegan Paul.

(2014). *Swift's Angers*. Cambridge: Cambridge University Press.

Refaie, Elisabeth El. (2009). Multiliteracies: How Readers Interpret Political Cartoons. *Visual Communication* **8**(2), 181–205. https://doi.org/10.1177/ 1470357209102113.

Robson, James. (2009). *Aristophanes: An Introduction*. London: Duckworth.

Ross, Trevor Thornton. (2018). *Writing in Public: Literature and the Liberty of the Press in Eighteenth-Century Britain*. Baltimore: Johns Hopkins University Press.

Rottman, J. (2014). Evolution, Development, and the Emergence of Disgust. *Evolutionary Psychology*, **12**(2), 417–33. https://doi.org/10.1177/ 147470491401200209.

Royzman, Edward, Pavel Atanasov, Justin F. Landy, Amanda Parks, and Andrew Gepty. (2014). CAD or MAD? Anger (Not Disgust) as the Predominant Response to Pathogen-Free Violations of the Divinity Code. *Emotion*, **14**(5), 892–907. https://doi.org/10.1037/a0036829.

Rozin, Paul, Jonathan Haidt, and Clark McCauley. (2008). Disgust. In Lisa Feldman Barrett, Michael Lewis, and Jeannette M. Haviland-Jones, eds., *Handbook of Emotions*, 3rd ed., New York: Guildford Publishing, pp. 133–51.

Rozin, Paul, Laura Lowery, Sumio Imada, and Jonathan Haidt. (1999). The CAD Triad Hypothesis: A Mapping Between Three Moral Emotions (Contempt, Anger, Disgust) and Three Moral Codes (Community, Autonomy, Divinity). *Journal of Personality and Social Psychology*, **76**(4), 574–86.

Russell, Pascale Sophie, Jared Piazza, and Roger Giner-Sorolla. (2013). CAD Revisited Effects of the Word Moral on the Moral Relevance of Disgust (and Other Emotions). *Social Psychological and Personality Science* **4**(1), 62–8. https://doi.org/10.1177/1948550612442913.

Ruthven, Malise. (1990). *A Satanic Affair: Salman Rushdie and the Rage of Islam*. London: Chatto & Windus.

Sams, Henry W. (1959). Swift's Satire of the Second Person. *ELH*, **26**(1), 36–44. https://doi.org/10.2307/2872078.

Scheer, Monique. (2012). Are Emotions a Kind of Practice (and Is That What Makes Them Have a History)? A Bourdieuian Approach to Understanding Emotion. *History and Theory*, **51**(2), 193–220. https://doi.org/10.1111/j.1468–2303.2012.00621.x.

Scully, Richard. (2018). Mark Knight vs Serena Williams – Crossing the Line: Offensive and Controversial Cartoons in the 21st Century. *International Journal of Comic Art*, **20**(2), 151–76.

Seymour-Ure, Colin. (2004). Low, Sir David Alexander Cecil (1891–1963), Cartoonist and Caricaturist. In *Oxford Dictionary of National Biography*. Oxford: Oxford University Press. https://doi.org/10.1093/ref:odnb/34606.

Shaftesbury, Anthony Ashley Cooper, 3rd earl. (1963). *Characteristics of Men, Manners, Opinions, Times Etc*. Edited by J. M Robertson (John Mackinnon). Gloucester, MA: PSmith.

Shakespeare, William. (2008). *Much Ado about Nothing*. Edited by Sheldon P. Zitner. Oxford: Oxford University Press.

Simpson, Paul. (2003). *On the Discourse of Satire: Towards a Stylistic Model of Satirical Humour*. Amsterdam: John Benjamins.

Snead, Jennifer. (2010). Epic for an Information Age: Pope's 1743 *Dunciad* in Four Books and the Theater Licensing Act. *ELH* **77**(1), 195–216. https://doi.org/10.1353/elh.0.0076.

Somanader, Tanya. (2014). President Obama Takes Over the *Colbert Report*. 2014. https://obamawhitehouse.archives.gov/blog/2014/12/09/president-obama-takes-over-colbert-report.

Spooner, John. (1999). *A Spooner in the Works: The Art of John Spooner*. Melbourne: Text Publishing.

Swift, Jonathan. (1999). *The Correspondence of Jonathan Swift, D.D.* Edited by David Woolley. Franfurt: PLang.

(2010). A Tale of a Tub *and Other Works*. Edited by Marcus Walsh. The Cambridge Edition of the Works of Jonathan Swift; 1. Cambridge: Cambridge University Press.

(2012). *Gulliver's Travels*. Edited by David Womersley. Swift, Jonathan, 1667–1745. Works. 2008; 15. Cambridge: Cambridge University Press.

(2018) *Irish Political Writings after 1725: A Modest Proposal and Other Works*. Edited by D. W. Hayton and Adam Rounce. Swift, Jonathan, 1667–1745. Works. 2008; 14. Cambridge: Cambridge University Press.

Swindells, Julia. (2014). The Political Context of the 1737 Licensing Act. In Julia Swindells, ed., *The Oxford Handbook of the Georgian Theatre*. Oxford: Oxford University Press, pp. 107–22. http://search.proquest.com/mlaib/docview/1986829610/89C880138FF24ED4PQ/2.

Tagar, Michal Reifen, Christopher M. Federico, and Eran Halperin. (2011). The Positive Effect of Negative Emotions in Protracted Conflict: The Case of Anger. *Journal of Experimental Social Psychology*, **47**(1), 157–64. https://doi.org/10.1016/j.jesp.2010.09.011.

Taylor, Craig. (2012). *Moralism: A Study of a Vice*. Durham: Acumen.

Taylor, Stephen. (2004). Walpole, Robert, First Earl of Orford (1676–1745), Prime Minister. In *Oxford Dictionary of National Biography*. Oxford: Oxford University Press. https://doi.org/10.1093/ref:odnb/28601.

Varey, Simon. (1993). The Craftsman. *Prose Studies: History, Theory, Criticism*, **16**(1), 58–77.

Warner, Michael. (2002). *Publics and Counterpublics*. New York: Zone Books.

Weinbrot, Howard D. (2005). *Menippean Satire Reconsidered: From Antiquity to the Eighteenth Century*. Baltimore: Johns Hopkins University Press.

Whelan, Frederick G. (2012). Burke on India. In David Dwan and Christopher Insole, eds., *The Cambridge Companion to Edmund Burke*. Cambridge: Cambridge University Press, pp. 168–80. https://doi.org/10.1017/CCO9780511794315.016.

Zekavat, Massih. (2017). *Satire, Humor and the Construction of Identities.* Topics in Humor Research, 6. Amsterdam: John Benjamins.

Zuroski, Eugenia. (2019). British Laughter and Humor in the Long 18th Century. *Literature Compass*, **16**(3–4). https://doi.org/10.1111/lic3.12521.

Acknowledgements

Satire and the Public Emotions depends in part on essays published elsewhere. I rejoice in the logic of this new Elements format particularly because it effectively saves the world from the republication of earlier work – no writer enjoys the revision and no reader needs to reacquaint themselves with work already published or found elsewhere. Consequently, I have kept repetition in this format to a minimum and gratefully acknowledge the editors and readers who helped me sharpen the ideas herein over a decade. Thanks go to all involved in 'Satire and the Limits of Literary Theories', *Critical Quarterly* 55:3 (2013), 44–58; 'The Emotional Contents of Swift's *saeva indignatio*', in Heather Kerr, David Lemmings, and Robert Phiddian, eds., *Passions, Sympathy and Print Culture: Public Opinion and Emotional Authenticity in Eighteenth-Century Britain* (Basingstoke: Palgrave Macmillan, 2016), 47–67; 'Spectacular Opposition: Suppression, Deflection and the Performance of Contempt in John Gay's *Beggar's Opera* and *Polly*', in Adam Morton and Mark Knights, eds., *Laughter and Satire in Early Modern Britain 1500–1800* (Woodbridge: Boydell & Brewer, 2017), 135–51; (with Jean McBain) 'Emotional and Scribal Communities in the *Verses on the Death of Dr. Swift*', *The Eighteenth Century: Theory and Interpretation* (58:3, 2017), 353–69. The Australian Research Council Centre of Excellence History of Emotions (project number CE110001011) supported some parts of the research. It has also been supported by internal funds and the gift of time from Flinders University.

While this Element is primarily a contribution to the study of Swift and his contemporaries, many of the arguments were honed in my parallel academic world, the study of Australian political cartoons. This taught me a lot about the limits of narrow literary approaches to satire and also of the wonders of co-authorship. So I particularly want to thank my collaborators in cartoons, humour, emotions, and culture's value: Jessica Milner Davis, Will Noonan, Khin Wee Chen, Ronald Stewart, Conal Condren, Sally McCausland, Liz Handsley, Michael Ewans, Murray Bramwell, Jean McBain, Heather Kerr, David Lemmings, Will Christie, Eric Parisot, Gillian Dooley, Suzy Freeman-Greene, Alex Cothren, David Olds, Richard Scully, Tully Barnett, Julian Meyrick, Diana Glenn, and Richard Maltby. My family environment keeps me sensitive to the satirical volatility of every meal and moment, so thanks and love to Robyn, Ellen, and Meg.

The Element is dedicated to my most persistent and robust collaborator, Haydon Manning of Politics at Flinders University. In a dozen publications and countless conversations, he has taught me that the really interesting questions about satire address its effects in the world. No doubt he will argue with much in these pages, and that is entirely as it should be.

Cambridge Elements ≡

Histories of Emotions and the Senses

Jan Plamper
Goldsmiths, University of London

Jan Plamper is Professor of History at Goldsmiths, University of London, where he teaches an MA seminar on the history of emotions. His publications include *The History of Emotions: An Introduction* (2015), a multidisciplinary volume on fear with contributions from neuroscience to horror film to the 1929 stock market crash, and articles on the sensory history of the Russian Revolution and the history of soldiers' fears in World War I. He has also authored *The Stalin Cult: A Study in the Alchemy of Power* (2012) and, in German, *The New We. Why Migration Is No Problem: A Different History of the Germans* (2019).

About the Series

Born of the emotional and sensory 'turns', *Elements in Histories of Emotions and the Senses* move one of the fastest-growing interdisciplinary fields forward. The series is aimed at scholars across the humanities, social sciences, and life sciences, embracing insights from a diverse range of disciplines, from neuroscience to art history and economics. Chronologically and regionally broad, encompassing global, transnational, and deep history, it concerns such topics as affect theory, intersensoriality, embodiment, human-animal relations, and distributed cognition.

Printed in the United States
By Bookmasters